MW00526506

Reflections of My Life
April March

The First Lady of Burlesque

Reflections of My Life

April March

The First Lady of Burlesque

Susan Baird

SHIRES ❦ PRESS
4869 Main Street
P.O. Box 2200
Manchester Center, VT 05255
www.northshire.com

Reflections of My Life

April March

The First Lady of Burlesque

©2016 by April March

ISBN: 978-1-60571-327-4
Library of Congress Number: 2016950341

No part of this book may be reproduced in any form or by any electronic
or mechanical means, without permission from April March.

Building Community, One Book at a Time
*A family-owned, independent bookstore in
Manchester Ctr., VT, since 1976 and Saratoga Springs, NY since 2013.
We are committed to excellence in bookselling.
The Northshire Bookstore's mission is to serve as a resource for
information, ideas, and entertainment while honoring the needs
of customers, staff, and community.*

Printed in the United States of America

Moshik Nadav Typography | www.moshik.net

This book is dedicated to my granddaughter Nicole,
my dearest friend Gerri Weise, and
to my friends, Grant Philipo and Craig Jackson.
They both have guided the revival of my career
with love and patience.

Also, to all my friends and fans,
my deep gratitude and love.
You made this project and my career possible.

Preface

It was June 2009 at the Miss Exotic World Pageant in Las Vegas. I was onstage doing a striptease for the first time in thirty-one years. I had been in burlesque for twenty-six years, from 1952 until 1978. And there I was at the age of seventy-five getting two standing ovations — again. And I loved it ever so much — again. So many wonderful memories and feelings came flooding back. The adrenaline was pumping and again I felt young and beautiful. A lot had happened during those years when I was little Velma Fern Worden from Oklahoma City. And a lot more happened in the sixty-plus years since Barney Weinstein renamed me April March and even since the 1960s when I was known all over the country as the First Lady of Burlesque. That's why I decided to write this book. I want to tell the story — as I remember it, in my own words. Just as I lived my life, I am going to do this *my* way. I hope you enjoy reading about it as much as I enjoyed living it. It was and continues to be quite a journey.

Foreword

April March. Two whimsical names. Reversed. Different. Playful. I didn't know they were attached to a woman who I would grow to cherish and honor. I first interviewed April back in 2010; in fact, she was one of my first burlesque stars that I was honored to interview and record their stories. I would go on to interview dozens (and dozens) more. But April's joy, honesty and sense of humor and real warmth made her a standout.

She wasn't a Velma, as she had been born, but like so many that found themselves pulled, inadvertently sometimes, into burlesque, April created the persona she identified with.

April was, and is, classy and elegant, with an eye on the past and the women who stripped before her and very much aware of the legacy she will leave.

A raven-haired beauty that looked remarkably like Jackie Kennedy, thus her moniker "The First Lady of Burlesque" though she never slept with JFK (and there were one or two of her contemporaries who claimed to). As her good friend and fellow stripper, Alexandra the Great 48 (aka Gerri Weise) told me "April suggested more with her eyes than she ever did with her body."

Dealing with many misconceptions about burlesque strippers, April proved them wrong by staying in her dressing room when not on stage, watching her soap operas. She wasn't running out misbehaving as most of the women I interviewed told me. Like April they were professional and spent their time preparing for their seven minutes on stage. Though April tried to push it with famed burlesque producer Harold Minksy telling him her act was thirteen minutes. He convinced April to pare down her act and leave them wanting more. She did and audiences indeed wanted more for a long time.

April is a romantic. Married as often as Elizabeth Taylor she sought the experience of falling in love. She has had suitors eating from the tips of her satin gloves; from the typical stage door Johnnies to King Saud of Saudi Arabia. Her story is incredible. She maintained her travails and triumphs with a wink in her eye, kindness in her heart and a generous spirit. She's a mother, a friend and teacher to many of the young women following in her footsteps today. She has left and will continue to leave her mark on this incredible art form, known as burlesque.

It is with my pleasure I present to you this long-overdue biography of this sensual, titillating woman, I call friend, April March.

Leslie Zemeckis
Author, Producer and Actress

I met April March, The First Lady of Burlesque, in 2012 and immediately fell for her spunky personality, wit and determination. These traits are what have allowed her to persevere in an industry and career that wasn't always full of glitz and glamour.

Being a burlesque star back in the 50's and 60's wasn't the easiest career path, but a life in showbiz beckoned and April answered the call.

With her signature look and elegant burlesque style, April became a headliner the moment she stepped on stage at seventeen years old. She was and still is a trailblazer for the performers that have followed in her footsteps. Not merely a legend of burlesque, but an icon. One of the very few who pioneered the seductive art of undress.

A life in show business, as many of you reading this book already know, is full of ups and downs and April certainly has had hers. But through it all she has endured and that's the most important part of chasing a dream.

Contrary to what some people believe, success isn't measured by fame and fortune, but by the impact you had on those you met while on your journey. And in that regard

April has accomplished more than most people ever will. Whether she realizes this or not, her courage and tenacity to strive for greatness and never give up on her dreams has inspired countless others to pursue dreams of their own and with that she has built an enduring legacy.

For those lucky enough to know April, whether through a fleeting moment at a burlesque festival or a lifetime of friendship, you've experienced a woman whose kindness, infectious laughter and youthful soul is a constant reminder that age is only a number and that taking the road less traveled, although at times difficult, always beats a life of safe mediocrity.

So with that, let April's story be a reminder that chasing a dream is not about attaining some definitive outcome. It's about having the guts to step out of your comfort zone and strive for greatness. The true payoff comes in knowing that you gave it your all and refused to settle for anything less than fabulous.

Craig Jackson
Producer and Cinematographer

It is not often that you get a chance to write about someone that you have admired for most of your life. I first saw April March perform over 55 years ago. It was a Saturday night at the Grand Opera House in St. Louis, Missouri. There were at least 1,000 people there waiting for the First Lady of Burlesque to appear. Suddenly, the lights dimmed and the curtains slowly opened. I saw her for the first time bathed in a lavender spotlight and a killer smile. She was easily the most beautiful woman I had ever seen. You could hear a sigh from the audience and I couldn't help but wonder what she was feeling surrounded by so much approval and adulation. It had to be overwhelming. Little did I know that I would have the same experience in the very near future? Many years later, I actually met April after one of my late night performances in Toledo, Ohio. This was the beginning of a very long friendship that has lasted to this day.

You are about to read about a true icon and an amazing survivor in the glamorous and sometimes not so nice world of Burlesque. Not many women in their eighties can still command a standing ovation. April can and when I witness this it is as if time stands still, and I am seeing her for the first time. The smile and magnetism are still there. And, the same adulation greets her as the curtain opens. This book is a true testament of a woman who has overcome the trials and tribulations of life and is still commanding the approval of her peers and the many who came after us. I am sure you will enjoy her story. It is amazing.

Gerri Weise (Alexandra the Great 48)
Burlesque Star and Entrepreneur

How do I write about a true Burlesque Legend? April March is the First Lady of Burlesque and so much more. I have been fortunate in my life to have met some really incredible people; April is at the top of this list. Being in male Burlesque, I never crossed paths with her, but I knew of her fame. Then, one day a dear friend invited me to have dinner with her. I instantly fell in love. Her charm is unmatched and her stories are priceless. From that moment, we have been great friends. She is not only stunning on stage but a genuine caring person. When she performs, she transports her audience back to when she was young and ruled the Burlesque stage. Her grace and beauty has traveled with her through the years.

When she asked me to accompany her on the Walk of Fame, I was surprised to learn that she gets nervous every time she goes on stage. She seems so calm. But, because of a recent injury I was concerned that she might fall. So, I took her hand in mine and guided her onto the stage. I really panicked since she was shaking so violently. I thought something was wrong and quickly escorted her off stage. Once in the wings, she looked at me very calmly and said that we were supposed to have made a circle. I told her that because of the shaking I thought something was wrong. She laughed and told me she was like that every time she goes on stage. Every time was like the first time. She is just that kind of person.

Shortly after that, she asked me to design her costumes. I was thrilled. She also introduced me once at an awards show and like a true trooper calmly read the very long introduction. My partner and I spend a lot of time with her and we always laugh and have a wonderful time. We so look forward to her every visit.

In 2015, I produced a number for her and had the music to "Roxy" from Chicago rewritten to honor this goddess of Burlesque. The audience went insane when the curtain opened. The smile on her face was magnificent and we all were transported back to the height of the Burlesque era.

There is something about April that immediately draws you in; she is your close friend right away. She uses these mesmerizing charms on everyone she meets, even audiences of thousands. A lot of performers hide behind a stage persona; but, with April you always get a real person. She may be draped in Jewels but it is April's true soul that you see first. Throughout her 80 years, she has faced many challenges and she still does. She faces them head-on and conquers them all.

I am so proud to call her my friend and to have witnessed the transformation of the past years as she turned herself back into the glowing beacon of joy and talent. Our museum staff and I cherish every minute we spend with her. She is more than a legend to us, she is our friend who we will cherish and love forever. Take some time now to learn about this wonderful lady by reading a small sample of her life stories. I am sure that you will pray that she will be willing to share more secrets in a second book.

Many people claim to be a legend, but April March truly is!

Grant Philipo, Owner and Operator
Las Vegas Showgirl Museum

Contents

Chapter One
Beginnings 1

Chapter Two
First The Gloves 23

Chapter Three
More Than The Gloves 35

Chapter Four
Love, Marriage, And Cyrese 57

Chapter Five
My Men: Some I Married And Some I Didn't 67
My Career In Photos 111

Chapter Six
So Many Wonderful Memories 127

Chapter Seven
The Other Side Of Burlesque 153

Chapter Eight
What Happened To Us All 177
My Name In Lights 197

Chapter Nine
The Rest Of The Story 207
The Burlesque Revival 223

Conclusion 241

Contents (continued)

Appendix
  My Husbands 243
  Burlesque Clubs I Worked 245
  April March Cocktail 249
  Historical Notes 251

Author's Note 257

Acknowledgments 259

Chapter One

Beginnings

Memories are wonderful, both good and bad. Together they form the stories of our lives. And both my story—and my life—have been good. I was born on June 18, 1935, a Tuesday, in Oklahoma City. I was a child of the Great Plains and of the Great Depression. My mother, Fern Lorraine Gragg, was the daughter of first-generation immigrants; my father, Clarence "Buddy" Worden, was a logger who had come to Oklahoma from West Virginia to seek his fortune. Together on that summer day, they named me Velma Fern.

They had met in Coeur D'Alene, Idaho in 1933. I am not sure how they met. Mom was exotic-looking and strikingly beautiful, due in no small part to her Cherokee blood.

Wherever she was, the boys would be hanging out. Because of the Depression, no one had money for traditional dating: the young people would just gather at street corners or in parks and drink bootlegged liquor or soda pops. Clarence Worden had been new in town when he joined the group. I imagine that my mother would have politely smiled at him and that he would have smiled back. His smile would have made him look cute: she'd be interested, but she wouldn't let him know it.

Buddy received his nickname because he was so friendly — and he was just as popular with the local girls as my mother was with the boys. They started dating in no time after meeting. Courtships and engagements were not long back then because of the economy. If you thought you loved someone, you married them quickly and simply. By the time of my birth, they had moved from Coeur d'Alene, Idaho to Oklahoma City, Oklahoma. There, my father got a job driving a Greyhound bus for a while. But theirs was not a love story made in heaven: four years later, they divorced. Mom and I immediately moved in with her parents. This was a journey that we would frequently make, from Coeur d'Alene to Oklahoma City; from our own house back to my grandparents. I got used to it, but from the time I was four my home was with my grandparents.

From then on, my father was pretty much out of my life. I don't remember him being there at all in my early childhood. He and Mother were divorced when I was just four, and I didn't see or hear from him again until I was sixteen. By that time, he had another wife, Mother was married to the fourth and last of her husbands, and I had already divorced my first. All by the age of sixteen! I don't remember anything about my father from those early years, and neither my mother nor my grandparents filled in the blanks. But I never asked them any questions. My mother was of average height, with beautiful blue eyes and gorgeous brown hair. Her Native American heritage made her exotic-looking. But beautiful as she was, she was self-centered and never paid much attention to me. It seemed that with all the drama in her life she just did not have the love or the time for the attention I needed.

My grandparents loved me so much, however, that I never blamed my mother or my father for not being there. My grandparents were so wonderful that there just weren't any voids or any anger. Although my mother sometimes sold real estate, most of the time she relied on my grandparents to support both of us when she was in-between marriages and houses; she relied on them to take care of me full-time when she wasn't. A couple of times after she remarried, I lived with her and her new husband. But this never lasted for long. My grandparents were the center of my life: they were my family. They adored me and I them, a mutual admiration that would last forever.

Papa was full Irish and Mam Mam was English and Native American (Cherokee.) They argued with each other all the time, but they loved each other even more. Supposedly, they never had sex after my mother was born. They were not demonstrative at all with others or each other. Still, they spoiled me rotten (just like grandparents are supposed to) and provided me with an environment more stable than whatever Mother could have created.

Papa always owned a small neighborhood grocery store when we lived in Oklahoma City. His was a "mom-and-pop," one-aisle, small-meat-counter kind of place — the sort of store where people used to shop in the days before supermarkets. My grandfather was a butcher by trade, so he worked behind the meat counter and helped my grandmother run the rest of the store. There tended to be a small house in the back: one bedroom, one bathroom, a small living room, and a kitchen. That's where we'd live. A couple of the houses we lived in over the years were a bit larger, but not much. When I wasn't in school or doing other things, I'd sit and have a soda pop or candy bar and just help them at the store. They were my best friends. My grandfather was a pillar of the community and received respect wherever we lived. My grandmother had wanderlust, though, which revealed itself in their frequent moves: when we were in Coeur D'Alene she wanted to be in Oklahoma City, and when we were in Oklahoma City she wanted to be in Coeur D'Alene. My mother had this trait, too: she always thought she would be happier on the West Coast, but when she was there she'd want to come back. And I have it, too, in that I'd always want to go back to burlesque no matter what "happy ever after" I'd found.

My grandmother, Ida, had three sisters. Nettie lived in Oshkosh, Missouri, but Minnie and her husband, Bode, still lived in Coeur d'Alene. So did Virgie, who had been deaf since childhood — a wonderful seamstress who held a position at the local cleaners. My grandfather, Elmer, had three brothers — Billy, Emmett, and Rufus — and they all lived in the Oklahoma City area. Like many couples back then, my grandmother ruled the roost. So even though my grandfather's grocery business always did well, if my grandmother was missing her sisters, Papa would sell whatever little store and house he owned at the time and we'd move back to Coeur d'Alene. He'd get a job as a butcher in one of the larger grocery stores, and she'd work as a presser in a laundry.

From the time I was very young, I wanted to be an actress. This was always my dream. Lots of little girls played with paper dolls in those days, but I only wanted ones of the famous stars of the time, like Alice Faye and Lana Turner. Since Mam Mam and Papa always got me what I wanted, I spent many happy hours in their small houses cutting out the latest glamorous outfits, folding over the tabs for that perfect fit, and acting out my childhood dream through those two-dimensional figures. Sometimes when I would get tired of dressing up my paper dolls, I'd dress myself up in Mother's clothing and jewelry and dance around for all three of them. I felt so elegant. They always applauded loudly at the end of my performances. My mother especially encouraged my dream, and never told me to stop the nonsense.

I also loved music and dancing. One of Papa's brothers, Billy Gragg, owned Blossom Heath, a large nightclub in Oklahoma City. Blossom Heath had it all: food, gambling (although it was illegal), dancing, and live music. *The* big bands of that era, like Ray Anthony, Woody Herman — bands of that caliber — played at Uncle Billy's place. Going to his elegant nightclub for the evening was a rare and special treat for my grandparents and me. Papa would wear his suit (the only one he had to his name) and Mam Mam would dress simply (as always.) But she'd roll my hair in rags earlier on those days to make Shirley Temple-like curls and dress me up in one of my prettiest dresses (with ruffles, of course) and shiny black patent leather shoes. Sometimes, even my white ankle socks would have ruffles on them. Then off we'd go, with Papa behind the wheel, Mam Mam beside him and me in the backseat. Mam Mam never learned how to drive and for a long time I thought women weren't supposed to drive.

I remember dancing with Uncle Billy: he always wore a white dinner jacket with a red carnation in the lapel. He was tall, good-looking, and very debonair. When I would stand on Uncle Billy's feet and glide around the dance floor to those big band tunes, I would say, "One day I'm going to be in show business." He would just laugh and continue dancing. But I was determined to be on stage.

My grandparents started paying for tap, ballet, and acrobatic dance lessons almost as soon as we moved in with them. Every week for seven years, they would drive me down to Katherine Duffy's small dance studio in Oklahoma City to perfect my skills on the bars and in the mirrors with the other girls in the class. I enjoyed all three forms of dance and the acrobatic lessons came in handy, years later, when a union executive challenged me to do a back-bend. But tap was always my favorite—and I was very good at it. In fact, it wasn't long before I expanded my show business dream to include becoming a professional tap and ballet dancer. But when Katherine approached my grandparents in 1946 to ask if she could take me with her to New York City, they refused. She had wanted to train me to dance on Broadway. And I was glad that they refused. They told her I was too young, and they were right—I was only eleven. I didn't want to leave Papa and Mam Mam: they were my home and safety and they were getting ready to move, too—back to Coeur d'Alene. I had just left Mother, her latest husband, Jack Hess, my stepbrother, Jackie (Jack's teenage son by a former marriage,) and my half-sister, Patty Jo, to again go to Idaho with them.

I was nine when Mother married Jack and I moved in with them and Jackie. What I remember most from the two years I lived with them was sitting and listening to my mother play her baby grand piano. Jack was an executive for the local electric company, a white-collar guy, so he had money. We had a beautiful home and Jack bought Mom the piano since she was an accomplished pianist. She could play any kind of sheet music you put in front of her, plus much more from memory. Sitting in that lovely living room with a fire in the background, just listening to her play — this is how I like to remember her and those years.

She also signed me up for music lessons and wanted me to learn how to play a musical instrument. I took violin for a brief period. But no matter how hard I tried, I just couldn't read sheet music. So Mom would mark my music with a marker to show me which finger to use to play each note. Our teacher, Mr. Faringer, eventually realized this and threw me out of the orchestra. He was no fun.

When I was ten, my mother took me to Will Rogers Park in Oklahoma City, where they were holding auditions for one of the 1945 "Our Gang" comedies. They were only casting for extras, so none of the current stars were there — but there were certainly a lot of other kids and their parents in the park that day. Since there were no speaking roles for the taking, the auditions were short and the whole thing — including the filming — only took a few hours. I never saw the finished version; I don't even know what the name of it was. But maybe, just maybe, if you take the time to watch all of the "Our Gang" shorts they made that year, you would spot Velma Fern Worden hanging out in the background with a group of the other kids. I was a skinny girl of average height, with medium-length, wavy jet-black hair. I was wearing light-colored shorts and a matching halter top. I had stars in my eyes. I still do.

I actually ended up meeting two of the "Our Gang" stars

years later. In fact, the first time I met Shirley Jean Rickert was in Oklahoma City. But by then, I was working as a burlesque dancer at Jake Samara's Derby Club. And the cute little blond girl with spit-curl bangs from the early-1930s "Our Gang" comedies was working at Jake's Jamboree Club, under the stage name "Gilda and Her Crowning Glory." I met "Spanky" McFarland — the chubby-faced, best-remembered leader of the Gang — in Tulsa, Oklahoma in 1957 at the Indian Hills Country Club where we were both members. We became such good friends and enjoyed talking about our pasts in show business.

A year after my movie debut, I was about as far away as you could get from the lights of Hollywood. I was just an eleven-year-old girl living on a farm in Coeur d'Alene, Idaho with her grandparents, trying to make new friends, again. Every time my grandparents moved from Oklahoma City to Coeur d'Alene or from Idaho back to Oklahoma — which , at the time, seemed like every couple of years — they had to start all over again, and so did I. We never moved during the school year, but it was still hard switching schools, not knowing anybody. It was hard to make friends; I made very few in either place. As soon as I finished the eighth grade, I quit school (which I hated.) I especially hated math: I wasn't good at it, and my teacher never missed an opportunity to humiliate me in front of my classmates. There was really no one at home to help me with homework since my grandparents had little formal schooling. Between all the moves and my lack of interest, I just wanted out—and my grandparents let me do it. I managed to get a job at a local drive-in as a car hop and earned a little income to help with my expenses. I was pretty cute in that little uniform and roller skates. It was a job of that generation and it was fun.

But even then, I loved to travel, and I loved those trips between Oklahoma and Idaho. I'd sit in the backseat, high atop a pile of blankets, and count the Burma-Shave signs on old Route 66, heading west, to pass the time. Or I'd count how many red cars or how many blue cars went by as we made our way south, back to Oklahoma City.

By the time I turned twelve, I finally had a best friend named Joyce Custer. Joyce was my first real friend. We would hang out together at the Coeur d'Alene Roller Rink. I *loved* to roller skate. They would hold racing contests every week, and I would always win. And then, Linda Bobbit started offering dance skating lessons at the rink. My grandparents—who always gave in to me—signed me up for lessons and began driving me back and forth between the farm and the rink once a week. I was good at that, too: I even did a solo. So I set my sights on becoming a professional roller skater— that is, up until the point when I fell head-over-heels for the boy Joyce's older sister was dating and set my sights on him instead. Female hormones at the age of thirteen are strong and determined. And was I *ever* determined.

My love's name was Benny Mitson. He was six years

older than me, a worldly nineteen when we met. He was very clean-cut and shy in a cute sort of way. He was a gentleman and *so* handsome and *such* a good skater and *quite* the popular young man. Of course, all the girls were after him. I couldn't understand why he was dating Joyce's sister of all people. She was a good skater and about the same age as Benny, but she was really skinny and had a flat-chest. And not at *all* pretty. So I said to myself, *"I'm* going to get him." And so I began my campaign to lure Benny away from his girlfriend. I even used my friendship with Joyce to spread rumors about Benny and me being "an item." Eventually, Benny and I started skating together, but only on occasion. He had about as big of a crush on his girl as I had on him, so for a long time, nothing happened.

It was a full house down on the farm in 1948. Mother moved that year from Oklahoma City to Coeur d'Alene with Patty Jo after she and Jack got a divorce. I was thirteen and Patty Jo was four; we each had our own bedroom. But soon, the house began to empty. Mother took over the role of taxi driver from my grandparents after she and my stepsister moved into the farmhouse. She would sit on the sidelines at the Coeur d'Alene Roller Rink and watch me skate while she waited for me to finish. That's where she met Chuck Lillard, her fourth and last husband. I was even the one who introduced them.

Chuck was one of the regulars at the rink. Benny and I would see him there just about every weekend. He was a very good skater. So wiry, he could twist his body around until he looked like a pretzel. But what made him really stand out was that he always wore a white shirt, suit, and tie when he skated. Benny and I thought Chuck was kind of crazy, but both he and Mother asked me to introduce them, so one night I did. Later, I couldn't believe it when Mother told me that they were dating. I was old enough to be appalled. "You can't do that! He's too young for you!" I told her (he was actually only seven years younger than Mother, but at the time I was sure he was at least ten.) "I can do whatever I want!" she replied. And before I knew it, Mother had married Chuck and she and Patty Jo had moved out of the farmhouse.

That's when Benny and Chuck became partners in a scrap metal business. Chuck didn't drive—didn't learn how to for years—but they bought an old pick-up truck so Benny could drive the two of them from Idaho to other states, like Montana and Wyoming to collect and sell scrap metal. It turned out to be a win-win situation. Benny and Chuck got a good price for the metal they collected. And because Chuck was married to my mother, I would see a lot more of Benny who was still dating someone else, despite the goo-goo eyes I sent his way than I would have otherwise. Their partnership came to an end when Chuck landed a job as a shoe salesman in Spokane, and he and Mother and Patty Jo moved from Coeur d'Alene to Washington. But by then, my campaign had ended and Benny and I were dating.

Benny split up with his girlfriend and every weekend

we would dance together to "Jealousy" and all those other romantic roller-skating tunes. We fell madly in love with each other. Well, he fell in love with me—I was already in love with him. And got him, I did. Marry him, I did. Just before I turned fifteen! It was about six months after Benny and I first started dating: I told Mother and Mam Mam that if they wouldn't sign for me to marry Benny (because I was underage,) I would run away and they would never see me again. Now, I always looked older than I was and I was very mature for my age. They gave in and in 1950 the four of us drove to nearby Sandpoint, Idaho, and Benny and I got married at a justice of the peace's office. The room was dark and dank and we had nothing fancy. I wore a little taupe suit with a peter pan collar and a white blouse. My long black hair tumbled down over my shoulders. It was just a simple, quick ceremony and we were husband and wife. But I was just a kid: when we got married, I still thought you could get pregnant from French kissing. Thank goodness Benny was six years older and knew a little more about sex than I did. Lovemaking was pretty awkward and surprising for me at first, but I adapted quickly and decided that I liked it. Good thing—considering what was to come.

My grandparents set up a makeshift room for us in their garage. It was not fancy and had a dirt floor. It was there that we spent our wedding night—no lingerie or champagne for us. I did have flannel pajamas, though. We were just two awkward kids trying to figure out what to do with each other. Imagine *The Grapes of Wrath* and that is pretty close to what our "room" looked like. When Mam Mam and Papa decided to sell the farm and move back to Oklahoma City, we found a nice little apartment in downtown Coeur d'Alene. This was our first place of our very own. I was feeling pretty grown up at that point. The only trouble was that since my grandmother had always done all of the cooking even after Benny and I got married, I never learned how to cook. Now I had to. Before she left, she told me that the marriage wouldn't last but that she hoped she was wrong. She said that Benny was a good man and wished us luck.

Benny got a job at a box factory and eventually so did I. But we were making boxes out of wood—not cardboard. We were measuring and cutting lumber on a huge round saw that was run by a noisy motor. It was very hard and very dangerous work, especially for such a young girl. But we were determined to make our own way, and we did. Neither his parents, an older couple who had two sons late in life, nor my grandparents supported us.

We were kids and playing house. It wasn't long before I started missing my grandparents—just like Mam Mam would start missing her sisters. So three or four months after Papa and Mam Mam left Coeur d'Alene, we did, too. I didn't have a license, but I'd been driving without one. I didn't know how to drive a stick shift; Benny taught me on the trip. So off we went to Oklahoma City in Benny's old Hudson, heading south, and then east, on Route 66. But this time, I wasn't sitting in the backseat on a pile of blankets, counting the Burma-Shave signs. This time, I was in the front seat next to my husband, just like Mam Mam. Or I was behind the wheel, like Papa, when Benny got too tired to drive anymore. I was all grown up and taking my place as the wife in our little story marriage.

We rented a basement apartment when we got to Oklahoma City. Benny got a job in one of the big grocery stores in town, making deliveries. Papa was working as a butcher at the same store because he hadn't found a little store of his own yet. But me? I was in that little basement apartment, cooking, cleaning, and playing the role of the stay-at-home housewife. I didn't like it and soon grew bored with playing that same role, day in and day out. I could feel myself getting more and more restless. I was also becoming attracted to other men. Benny wanted me to be a full-time housewife, but I still wanted to be an actress and to pursue my own dreams. Our hopes for the future were completely different.

Benny cried when I told him that I wanted a divorce. I think I broke the poor boy's heart. But I knew what I wanted, and I was used to getting it. So in 1951, just after I turned sixteen, Benny and I split up. I moved in with my grandparents— again. I was in-between marriages just like my mother for the first time. Papa had his own little neighborhood grocery store by then, and he and Mam Mam were living in the little detached house just behind it. I can still remember what street it was on: Northwest 10th.

I was sixteen when Papa sold his last little grocery store and he and Mam Mam finally settled down for good in Oklahoma City. They didn't have much money left by then, though, so they rented a little house. Too many years spent supporting my mother and spoiling me.

My father and his wife came for a visit around that same time. They stayed with Mother, Chuck, and Patty Jo who had left Spokane and moved to Oklahoma City. I never understood why my parents divorced and yet seemed so friendly when they saw each other. They stayed just long enough for my father to take me to Tulsa to meet his sister, Ruth Parmenter. I remember that she was married to a very prominent doctor. That was the first and last time I ever saw or heard from my Aunt Ruth. I didn't see my father again until I was twenty-one and vacationing in Miami Beach with my fifth husband.

When I was sixteen, I thought I knew everything I needed to know. More than anything else, I knew I wanted to be in show business. But I also knew I didn't want my grandparents to support me anymore. After I moved in with them, I went down to the *Daily Oklahoman* office and filled out an application for a job as a copy-girl. I lied about my age during the face-to-face interview. No one asked to see identification in those days and it helped that I acted very grown up for my age. I got the job.

I ran copy for the newspaper's reporters every day. Once

a week, I had to clean all of the brushes and glue pots in the office, and then go over to where they had the great, big barrels of yucky-smelling white paste and fill the pots back up again. I enjoyed running copy a lot more than cleaning, but since it was just a way to make money until I got my big break I decided to stick with it. That is until they sent me down to the Associated Press one day to retrieve the stock market information from the ticker tape machine.

There were three machines at the AP, and a man there showed me what to do. You had to put a small rubber thing on one hand and then tear off a piece of the ticker tape. But the tape came out so quickly that it all ended up in a big pile on the floor. The stock market information never made it from the floor at Associated Press into the *Daily Oklahoman* that day. When I was called to go up to the office of E.K. Gaylord himself—the elderly owner of the D.O.—I knew what I was in for. Before he had a chance to fire me, I walked up to him and said, "Mr. Gaylord, sir, I quit!" At least I was polite. Then I turned and walked out the door.

My next stop was the Derby Club. I knew that you had to be twenty-one just to go in and order a drink—and I was still sixteen. But I also figured that working at a nightclub would get me a lot closer to my show business dreams and a stage than running copy and cleaning glue pots. So I filled out an application for a job as a Cigarette and Flower Girl and interviewed with the club's owner, Jake Samara. I lied and said that I was twenty-one. Once again, I got the job.

Papa and Mam Mam didn't like the idea of me working at the Derby, even though they didn't know that it was a burlesque strip club (note: they *never, ever* saw me perform.) They also could never figure out how I managed to get the job in the first place. But what could they do? I would drive my grandfather's car into town even though I still didn't have a license. Every local policeman knew that I didn't have a license, but not one of them ever stopped me. I'd change from my regular clothes into one of my own cocktail dresses and walk around the club.

I usually got there around 8 PM and left between one and two the following morning. My job was to make up floral corsages and sell them—as well as cigarettes and cigars—to the customers. The salary wasn't that great, but the tips were usually pretty good since I was a pretty, young girl who enjoyed visiting and flirting with the customers. It was a safe environment since the Derby was an upscale dinner club and many of the customers had their wives or dates with them. So I felt perfectly safe flirting with the men. It was a good learning experience for my soon-to-be career.

At age 2, with my father Buddy
Worden in Oklahoma City.

A portrait of
Velma Fern Worden (1938).

In Oklahoma City at age 4.
Notice the smile is gone—
my dad had left.

My mother and me just before I started
school. When she was with us, she
made me feel special and loved.
Then, she would leave again.

At age 6, outside of my
grandparents' home.

With a friend in 1945.

ROLLER RINK TO CROWN "POPULARITY QUEEN"

Pictured above are the 12 candidates vying for the title of "Popularity Queen" of the Coeur d'-Alene Roller Rink. These girls are sponsored by 12 civic-minded local business firms, each presenting an award to the winning contestant. The varied gifts are on display at the Roller Rink now, C. J. Anderson, owner, announced. Left to right the girls are Marjorie Aresvik, sponsored by Tapley Cabinet shop; Velma Warden, Kost Shoe store; Barbara Hanson, DuBois grocery; Jackie Custer, Gay Shop; Opal Lee, Dr. Pepper Bottling company; Linda Bobbett, Norm' sRadio Shop; Irene Pfeiffer, Ben Franklin Store; Valle Joy Reisland, North Side Feed and Hardware; Barbara Cartwight, Marv's Service; Mary Lu Robinson, Dakin's Drive-In and Beverly Jones, Clara's Beauty shop. Not pictured is Shirley McCullum, Miller's Studio.—Coronation will take place at the Roller Rink, Wednesday evening, May 5.

I was named "Popularity Queen" at the roller rink just about a year
before I married Benny.

Patty Jo standing in front of my grandparents' store on NW 10th Street in Oklahoma City.

This is one of the houses where we lived in Oklahoma City, behind the store.

Mam Mam and Patty Jo in 1957.
I really loved them both.

Chapter Two

First the Gloves

The first time I ever saw a striptease show was on my first night at the Derby Club. After that, I'd watch the ladies perform every night. I was fascinated by their beauty and their gorgeous gowns and the artistry of their dances. I told myself I could *never* take *my* clothes off in front of people I didn't know. But I kept becoming more intrigued with the art of the dance. Little did I know that I would soon be on stage and that the stage would be my home for many years.

The dancers noticed my interest in their acts and started to take me under their wings. One would show me a dance; another would give me one of their boas. They all told me stories about performing in burlesque. My interest in the art of the dance increased.

There was an older man by the name of Keene Burwell that frequently came into the club. He was an oil tycoon and in a wheelchair. He took an interest in me but nothing improper; I think he felt sorry for me and the poor quality of my cocktail dresses. One day, he had his driver pick me up and he took me out to lunch. Afterwards, we went to Balliete's, a small boutique in Oklahoma City. He bought me the most beautiful clothes. One dress was a replicate of one that Joan Crawford had worn in a movie: it was ivory and had a jeweled top and a beautiful peau de soie swirly skirt. From that point on, I always loved full skirts that moved when I walked — I still do. He also bought me a fur stole to wear over my dresses. He was just a lovely man.

Opportunity knocks in different ways for different people. Sometimes it knocks politely and quietly: if you're ready, all you have to do is open the door and it is there, waiting for you to grab onto it. But sometimes it is right there waiting for you: for me, I literally ran right into it one night in the summer of 1951. It happened when I was rushing to the ladies room at the Derby Club and it came in the form of a balding, little gray-haired Jewish man that I almost knocked right on his rear.

After I hit him, I quickly apologized for nearly running him over. We quickly introduced ourselves. His name was Barney Weinstein. I told him that mine was Velma Fern Worden, giving him my full name. We chatted for a few minutes before he asked if I was on next. I laughed. I was astounded that he thought that I could be one of the dancers.

I had left my tray in the Cloak Room before heading to the ladies room, where I'd run into this poor man. I really had to pee and quickly get back out on the floor. "Oh, no! I could *never* do that! I could never take my clothes off in public! I'm the Cigarette and Flower Girl." I remember the conversation so well. The rest went like this:

"But with your looks you ought to be on stage! Haven't you ever wanted to be in show business?"

"Yes, that is what I want but I want to be a movie star."

"Well," Barney admitted, "I can't promise you movies. But I can start you in burlesque. I own a place in Dallas called the Theatre Lounge," he explained as he pulled a cardholder out of his pocket and handed one of the cards to me. "My brother, Abe, owns the Colony Club," he added.

"Hold on to that card, Oklahoma," Barney said, just before he left. "And if you ever change your mind, you come to Dallas and I'll get you in show business real quick."

I thought and thought about this. I asked some of the dancers at the Derby Club if they knew who Barney was. It turned out that some of them had worked for him in Dallas at the Theatre Lounge, and for his brother, Abe, too. They all liked him, his club and Dallas. A few weeks later, a photographer from *Look Magazine* was in the Club and asked me to do a photo shoot for him at a nearby lake, posing in a bathing suit. I did pin-up poses in a white bathing suit. I realized that I liked it and that wearing only a bathing suit in front of people at the park didn't bother me.

Still, I sat on Barney's offer for a few months and talked to Jake Samara and the dancers a lot about it. After a while, I convinced myself that taking off my clothes wouldn't be so bad. After all, I told myself, I wouldn't be taking off that much—it would be like posing in a bathing suit, which I had done once for the Look Photographer. Jake told me that Barney Weinstein had taken quite a few amateurs and turned them into big stars. Plus, it would be my chance to break into show business: Dallas was an exciting place to be—if I were really lucky, it would lead to a movie career.

I had to convince my grandparents to let me go to Dallas by myself. They didn't go out much. Their idea of entertainment was listening to the radio or watching TV. Also, I was certain that neither of them had ever seen a striptease show, or ever would. But they definitely knew how much I loved to dance after taking me to lessons for all those years, and I knew they'd remember Katherine Duffy's offer to train me as a professional Broadway dancer back when I was eleven. So I told them that I had been offered a job in Dallas—as a tap dancer. Reluctantly, they agreed to let me go: they knew I was going to do what I wanted to do, anyway. Besides, by that time I had already been married and divorced. I wasn't a child and they didn't have much control over me even when I *was* a child.

So I packed a couple of suitcases—including my old tap dance costume—and my grandparents drove me to the Greyhound depot in downtown Oklahoma City to see me off. But not before lecturing me about taking care of myself and watching out for strange men and keeping in touch. And not before my grandmother cried, a lot. "Mam Mam, I'm going to be famous star someday," I told her. Then on the bus I got and off to Dallas I went.

As soon as the Greyhound arrived, I got off the bus and into a cab and read off the address listed on Barney's business card. Dallas was hot and sprawling. I was excited and scared, asking myself if I really could do this. I talked to myself during the ride, telling myself that I was stupid one minute and convincing myself that I could do it the next. The address was a ways outside of the city and in a commercial block. The door to the Theatre Lounge was open, so once inside I headed straight for the one room with a light on, which turned out to be Barney's office. I poked my head in, unannounced. "Well, well! Oklahoma! I knew you'd eventually get here! Welcome to our family!"

I was nervous and afraid that I would quickly lose my courage. I didn't have time for pleasantries; I had a question that needed answering right away. "So", I blurted out, "do I have to take a lot of clothes off?"

"No. Not that many," Barney reassured me. "The other girls will just tell you what to do. You will know what to take off and when. And Halloween, one of the other dancers and the club's seamstress, will make you a costume." Halloween and I had met at the Derby Club and I was glad to see a familiar face.

He said he would talk to the band and arrange for me to start rehearsing the next day. He asked if I had any money and I told him that I did. Barney called a nearby hotel — one that charged "theatrical" (reduced) rates to entertainers performing in the area — and arranged a room for me. Then after writing down the address and room number on a card and handing it to me, he called a cab, paid the fare in advance, and off I went. I can't remember the name of the hotel anymore, but it was a nice place with a clean room. Early the next afternoon, I caught a cab back to the Theatre Lounge to start rehearsing my routine.

I never signed a formal contract with Barney, but he paid me — I think it was $85 a week — to perform. And not long before my opening night, he took me to the local American Guild of Variety Artists (AGVA) office so I could pay my dues and get my union card (yes, you needed a union card to work in burlesque!) Barney told me that I couldn't perform unless I joined the union. But what he didn't tell me was that I'd have to perform *before* I did.

A man named Vincent Lee was the union representative of the Dallas branch of AGVA at that time. He asked me what made me think that I was qualified to call myself a performer. I told him I had taken tap, ballet, and acrobatic lessons for years. He answered by asking me to do a back-bend. I didn't see what doing a back-bend had to do with getting my union card, but I did one anyway (a perfect back-bend, I might add.) I thought that would be the end of that.

But then Mr. Lee asked how old I was. I was only sixteen, and knew that wasn't going to work. If I told him I was eighteen, though—which was the legal age at that time— it might have made him suspicious. I decided it would be better to jump up one from there. So I told him I was nineteen. End of conversation. I was in the union.

When I started at the Theatre Lounge, Artie Brooks was the comic/MC and Debbie Dean—who performed a complex routine dressed in a half-devil/half-virgin costume—was one of the dancers. I thought Debbie was married to Artie, but that's another story for later. Sharon Sutton worked as a dancer there, too, along with Halloween and several other ladies whose names, unfortunately, I've forgotten. The small house band played for all of the performers, who were all very nice to me. Back then, performers didn't treat each other like competitors: they stuck together and looked out for each other.

It took about three days for Halloween to make my costume. It was a two-piece draped outfit—a sleeveless top and a long skirt, with a zipper in the back of each. It was rose-colored with silver stripes. Of course, I also wore a pair of long, black gloves. Whenever I do interviews, they always ask me what I take off first. My response is always the same: "A lady always removes her gloves first."

I developed my routine during the following two weeks when I rehearsed with the band. Sometimes Barney would stop by to watch my rehearsals but he usually just stayed in his office. Even when he did stop by, he never told me what to do. And the only instructions the girls gave me were to "go out and dance and take things off." So I ended up just doing my own thing.

My final routine was a little dance, a little shimmy with a few bumps and grinds, and walking up and down the short runway. I think back then, the whole routine must have lasted fifteen minutes or so. It started out with a pretty song (pretty songs are my favorites.) But after the band finished playing all the "April" tunes they knew, like "I'll Remember April" and "April in Paris," I danced to things like "Ballin' the Jack" and "I Wish I Could Shimmy Like My Sister Kate."

I was *very, very* nervous waiting in the wings to go on stage on opening night. It was a packed house—maybe eighty people—and I had overheard one of the waitresses say that all of the lead cast members of *Guys and Dolls* had come to see the show that night and had a table ringside to the runway. Their road show was at the Texas State Fair and their performers frequently visited the local clubs.

Artie Brooks introduced me: "Miss April March." Barney told me I needed a new name the day I showed up at his office. He explained that Velma Fern Worden wouldn't look good on marquis. I can still remember how he ran down the aisle a few days after I started rehearsing, so excited that he had a name for me. "I've got it! I've got it!" I asked what he had. Your new name, he responded. Now he had my attention. I asked what it was.

He said that my name should be "April March." I wasn't impressed: I reminded him that March comes *before* April. Not in your case. You look so spring-like and summery. You're a breath of fresh air…You just look like an April," he declared. Finally, I agreed. So April March I became and April March I stayed. Through all the years, most of the girls changed their names two or three times. But I only changed mine that once.

The audience began to applaud loudly as soon as I walked on stage that first night — and they kept it up the whole time. But I was still nervous and unsure of myself. Artie had announced that this was my debut performance. I thought that maybe they were applauding out of sympathy for me because I was doing so badly.

I had rehearsed the first part of what the other girls had told me to do — the part about going out on stage, and the part about dancing. I had even taken the time to put on false fingernails to hide my short ones before putting on my gloves so that I'd look more sophisticated. But I'd never rehearsed the part about taking off clothes. I was still reluctant to do it and I chose to forget about doing it.

The runway was relatively short, so at first I spent most of my time dancing on the stage itself. All of the other dancers were stationed behind the curtain, ready to coach me on what to take off next when I danced over by them. But I was on stage for several minutes before one of the girls finally realized what was happening — or should I say, *not* happening—and called out from behind the curtain that I had to take something off!

I took off my gloves (First mistake) and was on the runway, fumbling to unzip my top (Mistake #2) when one of my fake fingernails popped off my finger and landed in a nearby customer's glass. I kind of saw where it landed, but more than anything else I heard it—and so did everyone else. It was a loud *PLOP*. That's when the laughter erupted—from a table ringside to the runway, just to my left—and it spread like wildfire until everyone in the place was laughing.

Everyone except me, I was so embarrassed that I didn't know what to do. The last thing I remember is running offstage and into the dressing room—vowing never to return to any stage again. So when the waitress came backstage to tell me that the cast of *Guys and Dolls* wanted me to join them at their table, I told her I just couldn't. I was too embarrassed to show my face. "But, April! It's the cast of *Guys and Dolls*!" she repeated.

She was right, of course. These were the Broadway stars, on their first national tour! They'd only be in town at the Dallas State Fair for a couple of weeks. How could I pass up an opportunity like that? So I agreed to come out. It wasn't until I followed the waitress down the stage stairs and approached their table—ringside to the runway, off to my left—that I saw the looks on their faces and realized exactly where that fake fingernail had landed. By then, it was too late to turn and run. But I wanted to.

They told me what a great job I had done for my first time on stage. They introduced themselves as "Slapsie" Maxie Rosenbloom (former world light heavyweight boxing champion turned Hollywood character actor, who was playing the role of "Big Jule" on tour,) Julie Oshins (aka "Nathan Detroit",) Dave Starr ("Harry the Horse",) and last (but definitely not least) Ray Shaw (Allan Jones'/"Sky Masterson's" understudy.) The minute I saw him I fell in love. He was like Benny all over again, only stronger. Wow, I thought he was so good-looking—and the chemistry was there-- big time.

Then Maxie took my hand. "Everybody sure got a big laugh when your fingernail landed in my glass," he said as one of the other "guys" pulled out a chair and motioned me to take a seat at their table. "But April—*nobody's* going to pay any attention to your short fingernails when you're on the stage. So if I were you, I wouldn't wear those false ones anymore."

And I never did. But my debut was over and I was a burlesque dancer, sort of. If only I had taken off some clothes! At that point, I never could have imagined the future I would have on runways across the country. Burlesque wasn't even my ambition or goal. I still wanted to be an actress. But now, I also wanted to get to know Ray Shaw better. I vowed that I would do both.

At age 11, in the dancing costume that I brought to Texas to convince my grandparents that I was looking for a job as a dancer. Sort of true.

In 1952, one of my first burlesque costumes. It was made by Halloween, one of the other dancers. It was a Kelly green satin with sequin trim. I was all of 17. (I can't explain the hat, really. I guess I didn't develop a fashion sense until much later.)

Chapter Three

More than the Gloves

G oing to a burlesque show was like going to a nightclub. The Master of Ceremonies/Comedian performed jokes and little skits and the girls danced to well-known songs. Often there would be dancing between numbers: many men would bring their wives or groups would come for a night's entertainment. Sure, some men came to make goo-goo eyes at the girls, but most customers just wanted a night out and some entertainment.

Later that first night, I went on for my second number. I was more than a little nervous, but the other girls stood behind the curtains and coached me so that I'd make it through. They told me what to take off when and made me feel much more at ease on the stage. You were never completely naked. You basically went down to your underwear which consisted of a net bra with pasties on your nipples and net panties that were reinforced in the important areas. The crowd again cheered me on; I actually enjoyed strutting up and down the runway. My career had officially launched.

The cast of *Guys and Dolls* played at the Dallas State Fair from October 6 through the 21st. After they came to see my debut at the beginning of their two-week run, we all went to breakfast just about every night once I finished my last show. I got to know them pretty well, but I *really* wanted to get to know Ray Shaw—that tall, handsome guy in his late-twenties or early-thirties with the black hair and mustache who I fell in love with at first sight. We went out alone just a few times, and during those times he treated me like I was the only woman in the world for him. That's why I was only too willing to go to bed with him. And I did. He was my second lover and much more worldly than Benny.

Dave Starr warned me about Shaw. He told me bluntly that he was a real womanizer who had a girl in every town in which the show performed. I was sure that Dave was wrong. *Oh, that's not going to happen with me!* I said to myself. *He's going to fall in love with me.*

But I was the one who was wrong, was I ever! You know that old saying, "out of sight, out of mind"? Well, that's what happened. When *Guys and Dolls* left Dallas, I was out of Ray Shaw's sight and out of Ray Shaw's mind. I was totally heartbroken.

I wondered how I ever could have let myself be so foolish as to fall in love with somebody like that so quickly. I asked myself this over and over again. He must have thought I was just a green kid that didn't know any better. I was, but I was obsessed with him and thinking about him all the time. But, I went on. I did take Maxie Rosenbloom's advice and never wore false fingernails again on stage. Yet I didn't stop searching for other ways to look more sophisticated or to find a stage gimmick. This is why one afternoon in downtown Dallas I stopped in a tobacco shop that sold all kinds of foreign, fancy cigarettes.

I looked around for a bit, but the minute I saw a long, green velvet box with long, pastel cigarettes with gold tips I knew I *had* to have them. *These would be very elegant for me to smoke on stage*, I said to myself. The owner tried to warn me about them, saying that they were very strong Turkish cigarettes. But I was smoking Pall Malls at the time, and I didn't think these would be that much stronger. So I bought them and took them with me to the club that night. In between shows, I lit one up in the dressing room. The taste was so strong it made me cough, and the odor was so strong it made me gag — and it went through the entire club.

At that point, Barney came running into the dressing room to ask if I was smoking pot.

After I caught my breath, I told him that I didn't know what pot was or smelled like. "But I'm smoking a Turkish cigarette. Isn't it pretty?" Barney was not impressed and told me to get rid of them and never smoke them in his club again. So there went my new gimmick and my sophisticated Turkish cigarettes.

It definitely took me a lot longer to get over losing Ray Shaw than those sophisticated-looking cigarettes. But not *that* long. By the time the Sonja Henie Ice Show rolled into town, I managed to pick myself up, dust myself off, and meet another guy—one of the ice skaters with the show. He was a nice, sweet boy from California named Andy Vercheck.

We dated for the couple of weeks that the show was in Dallas. He took me out to eat and watch a couple of the rehearsals. He introduced me to Sonja Henie, who had a vulgar mouth like Judy Garland (I didn't meet Judy for years, but that's a story for later.) Because I didn't get attached to Andy like I did Ray Shaw, I wasn't heartbroken when he left town with the show. I did manage to "lose" a yellow Cadillac convertible in the process, though.

It all started at the Theatre Lounge one night, when Barney introduced me to a Texas oil millionaire after I finished my act. I can't remember his name, but I remember thinking at the time that he drank a lot. When he asked if he could take me shopping at Neiman Marcus the following day, however, I didn't hesitate to say "yes." I had never been there before, and I knew that their main store was located in Dallas. When I asked if I could bring my friend, Linda Powers, with me, he was quick to say "yes" as well.

Linda and I first met at the Derby Club in Oklahoma City when she was a twenty-something burlesque dancer and I a sixteen-passing-for-nineteen-year-old Cigarette and Flower Girl (her real name was Betty Grabbe.) She was a short, petite girl — under five feet tall — with short, curly platinum hair and big blue eyes. She didn't do much on stage; she just danced around a bit. She had very small breasts for someone in burlesque, but Linda was so cute. We became friends, and not long after I debuted at the Theatre Lounge, Linda came to Dallas, too. We worked at the Theatre Lounge and later on at the Derby Club together for several months. Years later, she would marry Ray Price, the country western singer.

You can imagine how thrilled Linda was when I told her that the two of us were going on a shopping spree the following day — and at Neiman Marcus! Not to mention that an oil millionaire I'd just met that night was bankrolling it! We were ready and waiting when the cab pulled up in front of our hotel the next day, courtesy of the millionaire, of course. When the cab arrived at Neiman Marcus, both he and Mr. Stanley Marcus were waiting in front of the store to greet us. They escorted us inside and up the stairs to the designer clothes section.

I felt just like a famous movie star. A sterling silver tea set was placed on a nearby table in a private salon so that Linda and I could drink tea and nibble on small pastries while the models modeled dozens of beautiful outfits for us to choose from. Mr. Marcus treated us like two of his regular rich customers. I'm sure the millionaire was making a play for me, but he seemed content to just sit there drinking bourbon out of a silver flask, watching one excited young girl try on a lot of clothes and then model them in front of him.

Linda ended up getting a suit, a blouse, a pair of alligator shoes, and a bag that cost over $5,000. By the time I had picked out my last outfit, more than four hours after we first arrived, I had over $250,000 worth of clothes. After everything was boxed up, I gave the millionaire a kiss on the cheek and told him that I would see him at the Theatre Lounge that night. With the boxes and boxes of designer clothing loaded into the cab, Linda and I made our way back to the hotel.

Unbeknownst to me, that same millionaire had yet another surprise in store for me. He ordered a yellow Cadillac convertible to be delivered to the club that night. It even had a big, red ribbon on it, Barney told me later on. But I had a date with Andy Vercheck, and snuck out the back exit to meet him after my last show.

Needless to say, I never saw the oil millionaire again — and I didn't get the car. But I still wound up with a ton of beautiful designer clothes that he paid for before Linda and I left Neiman Marcus that day. It was the first and last shopping spree that that particular oil millionaire had paid for, but it turned out to be only the first of many, many more in my long career in burlesque. It seemed like everyone wanted to take me shopping for clothes, jewelry, furs, and cars. I reveled in the attention. I was a very spoiled young woman:

to some extent, these men continued what my grandparents had started — they gave me everything I wanted.

About a month after the oil millionaire, the yellow Cadillac with the red ribbon, and Andy Vercheck disappeared, a waitress came back to my dressing room between shows to tell me that a handsome young man wanted me to join him at his table. As it turned out, he was an actor named Charles Braswell. The waitress had not been exaggerating: he was one of the most *handsome* men I had ever seen. We spent a lot of very romantic evenings together over the next several months — that is, until he got a call from Hollywood for a screen-test in a movie with Elizabeth Taylor. "Sweetheart, I'll call you and I'll write to you and we'll see each other soon," he promised before he left. He did call me for quite some time afterwards. Ultimately, however, he remained in California, and that was the end of Charles Braswell.

While I was performing in Dallas, I was aware that the Weinstein brothers were having financial problems with the IRS. It seemed that another club owner — one Jack Ruby — kept filing complaints that claimed that they were underreporting income. This wasn't true: Ruby's agenda was to put them out of business. One day, one of the other girls and I walked by the Carousel Club; curious, I asked her about it. She said that it was owned by Jack Ruby, a real "sleaze". She told me to stay away from him because everyone knew he was trouble.

By then, it was 1952 — the year that both my professional and personal life took a major turn. This was the year when *everything* seemed to happen. Early that year, I had my first out-of-town engagement: my agent, Chick Scoggins (the first agent I ever hired,) got me the booking. It would last two weeks at Matin's Melody Lane in Houston, Texas with star billing. But I would have to perform two different numbers: my regular burlesque act and a tap dance routine. To make a name for yourself, you had to go on the road — and on the road I went.

Chick told me about the booking in late-1951, so I had some time to prepare. It had been awhile since I had taken tap dance lessons from Catherine Duffy back in Coeur d'Alene — and the routines I had learned back then were meant for children. So I contacted Billy Taylor, an African American tap teacher I had met at a tap school as a young girl, to arrange for private lessons. He taught me a routine to "Lullaby of Broadway." After about a week of rehearsing, I felt I was ready. And I must have been right, because my two-week engagement at Matin's Melody Lane got held over for four more weeks. It was a great start to a new year — with two notable exceptions.

The first exception occurred the evening Ted Lewis came to Matin's Melody Lane, quite drunk, and sat at a front-row table. As soon as I came on stage and started my tap dance routine he started booing me. And he wouldn't stop. I ran off the stage in tears; I really was still a child. When Mr. Matin came backstage to ask me what was wrong, I gave him an earful.

"That man out there is *nasty*! He's *very* drunk, and he booed me off the stage. I want you to get him to leave, because I don't want to perform again until he's out of the club."

"I can't do that, April," Mr. Matin explained. "That's the famous Ted Lewis."

At the time, I didn't even know who Ted Lewis was. As it turns out, he was a famous entertainer and band leader who got his start back in the 1920s; he was best known for his catchphrase, "Is everybody happy?" At the time, all I knew was that I was anything but happy — thanks to him. Mr. Matin did his best to calm me down. "I'll go over and talk to him, April, while you get ready to do your second number." So that's what I did.

After I finished my strip number — I didn't get booed — I went back to my dressing room. But as soon as I got dressed, I went back out and headed straight for the table where Ted Lewis sat. "Mr. Lewis, sir, you're *very rude* and I want you to leave, immediately." He didn't respond; he just sat there looking at me. But at least I had the satisfaction of telling him what I thought of him to his face.

The second incident also involved someone famous — and horribly drunk. One evening, I returned to my hotel after my last show at Matin's to find that the electricity was out. Since I couldn't take the elevator and my room was on the 17th floor, I decided to just sit in the lobby and wait until the electricity came back on. Not long after I had found a seat by the window, in walked a *very* drunk Bob Wills, the famous lead country-western singer of Bob Wills and The Texas Playboys. The minute he saw me, he came over and started making passes at me, leaning over and trying to kiss and hug me. I asked him to stop several times but he didn't. Finally, I gave him a shove—and he fell backwards into the big plate-glass window and it broke. That caused quite a stir. Just as the two men from behind the front desk were picking him up and sitting him in a chair, the electricity came back on. So I got up, walked over to the elevator, pushed the button, got in, and went up to my room. I never saw Bob Wills again. And I certainly wasn't a fan of his after all that.

After my otherwise successful six-week engagement in Houston, I headed back to Dallas to work at the Theatre Lounge. As I said earlier, a young fellow by the name of Artie Brooks— another very handsome young man—was the comic/MC there. He developed a big crush on me, but I still thought he was married to Debbie Dean, one of the other burlesque dancers at the Theatre. I flatly refused to date him. "But I'm not *married* to her," Artie tried to explain. "I'm just *living* with her." When I said, "Well, that's the same thing," that was the end of that conversation—until I left Dallas for two bookings in Oklahoma City and Artie followed me. This was the first time I returned home as April March.

My first booking was at the Gaiety Theatre. After that, I started working at Louie's 29 Supper Club for Louie Strauss, the very kind, elderly, white-haired gentleman who owned the place. Red Ford was the comic there at that time. He did an act called "Red Ford for President," and also a funny "drunk" act. He was an older gentleman—in his sixties, I believe. I worked with Red quite a bit at Louie's. Once back in Oklahoma City, I saw my grandparents for the first time since leaving home. By then, they knew that I was in burlesque, though I am not sure that they knew what burlesque was. They never came to my shows and I preferred it that way.

When Artie told me that he had broken up with Debbie, we started dating. But when he went back to Dallas to work at the Theatre Lounge, I stayed on in Oklahoma City for four weeks, starring at Louie's 29 Club, until I got booked into the T-Bone Supper Club in Wichita, Kansas for two weeks.

I hired Eleanor Vaughn and Ruth Sallee as my agents when I returned to Oklahoma City. Either one or the other booked me all around: in Oklahoma City, Kansas City, Wichita.... I actually didn't travel that much, or work in that many places in all those years. Everybody kept bringing me back, so I guess they liked me. I was building quite a reputation.

Artie came to Wichita to see me while I was working at the T-Bone, but by then I had met and was dating a German test pilot by the name of Hans, so that was the end of our relationship. Hans was a wonderful lover; we had such a romantic time together that I was sad to see him leave. Many years later, however, Hans saw my ad in the paper when I was working at the Palace Theatre in Buffalo and came to see me. Needless to say, we picked up our love affair again. As

I said, he was a *great* lover, but also a married one: our little fling only lasted a few days.

I continued to get booked for engagements at Louie's 29 Club when I returned to Oklahoma City from Wichita. But thanks to Ruth Sallee, I also started working for Jake Samara again—this time, however, as a burlesque star instead of a Cigarette and Flower Girl.

I was working at Louie's 29 Club when I had a short, romantic affair with Monte Hale—a tall, handsome guy with blue eyes, sandy hair, and a great body. He was a famous cowboy-western movie star at the time: there were even Monte Hale comic books, just like those that featured Roy Rogers and Gene Autry. We were still dating when I got a two-week booking in Las Vegas—New Mexico, not Nevada. In his yellow Cadillac that had a gun as the gearshift Monte drove me down to the train station in Oklahoma City, gave me one of his comic books, and said his farewells just before he put me on the train:

"Sweetie, you're going to Las Vegas, New Mexico and I'm going to Dallas. Here's the number of the Adolphus Hotel, where I'll be staying. Give me a call when you get to Las Vegas and you get settled and everything, and we'll keep in touch."

If I had known what I was getting into, I never would have gotten off the train in Las Vegas.

The "nightclub" at which I was booked for two weeks was a cowboy joint. The owner's office was my "dressing room," and the band couldn't read music—the only tune they could play was "Mexicali Rose." Without other options, I did my routine to "Mexicali Rose." After I finished my show and two or three encores — to the same song, I was ready to get offstage, go into my "dressing room," and change into my clothes. The audience was hootin' and hollerin', but there was nothing else I could take off — legally, anyway. In any case, I wasn't about to do so. But the owner wouldn't let me off the stage: he had two holstered guns, and when I tried to leave he drew both of them and told me to stay out there and entertain the cowboys. So I stayed out there: I did a few more encores to "Mexicali Rose" and then I ran like hell to escape.

This was the first and not the last time that I would run for my life. The owner drew his guns again, but I guess I managed to get past and outran him. As soon as I got in his office, I slammed the door shut and bolted it. Then, somehow, I dragged the big, heavy oak table in his office over to the door and shoved it up against it. After I got dressed and packed up all my things, I opened the office window, threw the luggage out, and climbed out after it. Off I went down the road, carrying that luggage, hitchhiking into town, and vowing never to return to Las Vegas, New Mexico *ever again.* When I finally got to the hotel, I decided to call Monte Hale at the Adolphus and tell him what had happened.

Monte wasn't pleased to hear from me. He was angry that I called and told me not to call him that late at night anymore! Convinced that the operators would listen in, he worried that word would get out about our affair. He thought it would be bad publicity for him. His advice was to get in touch with my union representative and ask him what to do. So that's what I did.

I called Vincent Lee in Dallas: it was 2:30 in the morning by then, so I had woke him up. I was crying, but I managed to tell him the gist of the story. "What am I to do? I'm not going back to that club!" He told me that under the circumstances, I didn't have to. He told me to buy a ticket and take the first bus out of Las Vegas. And that's what I did—I got out of Dodge as soon as I could.

I *never* returned to that Las Vegas again. I did, however, return to New Mexico a few weeks later for a booking in Raton. What a contrast! The club was small but very nice, and the couple who owned the club was lovely, warm, and welcoming. I enthusiastically looked forward to opening night. My opening performance was set to "Spellbound." I came out on stage, did three or four spins, and was about to go into my dance when...I collapsed! By the time I came to, I was backstage and a doctor was attending to me. Some of the customers had taken me off stage and laid me in a booth, and luckily a doctor and his wife were in the audience. After he checked me out, he gave me the bad news: he told me that I had to go to the hospital and have my tonsils removed right away. He was afraid that they were going to burst.

I had had problems with tonsillitis when I was a child, but I was scared to death to have surgery and refused to get them taken out. "You *have* to go," he insisted. So the next morning, alone, I took a taxi to the local hospital in Raton to have my tonsils taken out by the same doctor who had come to my opening night performance. Some opening night that was! In those days, they blindfolded you and had you sit in a chair, but I could see underneath the blindfold. Lo and behold, one of the tonsils burst. When I saw all the blood, I started to gag. "Don't gag!" the doctor said. "Don't move. Don't do anything."

The two days I spent in the hospital made front-page news in Raton, "Burlesque Star in Hospital for Tonsillectomy." "Burlesque Star Released from Hospital." I really didn't like this kind of publicity, but everyone told me that any publicity was good for my career.

By the third day, I figured that I had to try to go to work. When I asked the doctor, he told me that I really shouldn't; I was too weak. However, he said that if I *had* to go back, he would write me a prescription for some Dexedrine. He said that I should always drink water and other liquids out of the glass straw they had given me when I left the hospital. So before I went to work that night, I took two Dexedrine — and believe me, when that taxi pulled up in front of the hotel I could barely feel my feet touch the ground! When I got to the club, the owners told me how happy that they were to have me back…but they told me to take it easy.

So, I took it easy, I sat at the bar and sipped water through a glass straw until it was time to go back and get ready for my show. Even though I was still flying high on Dexedrine, I managed to get dressed and get out on the stage. But halfway through my act, I collapsed, again. I was making quite a name for myself by collapsing yet another time in the same city.

Unfortunately, there was no doctor in the house that time, but somebody in the audience got a shot of whiskey, lifted up my head, and poured it down my throat. Well, believe me, that whiskey revived me quickly. Oh my goodness gracious, it *really hurt*! I still remember it so clearly. I continued to work after that until the end of my scheduled engagement. But even though I missed a total of four nights, the owners paid me for the full two weeks. Then I was off on a bus to El Paso, Texas for a booking in Juarez, Mexico.

When the bus arrived in El Paso, I took a cab and checked in at the Hilton Hotel. Then I went to the office of Ross Valore, the agent who booked me in Juarez. That night, he took me over the bridge where you have to declare your citizenship to go into Mexico. I worked several clubs in Juarez during the next two weeks, including The Tivoli Club and The Follies. I don't remember which club we went to that first night, but I remember that it was very dark inside; I thought to myself, *Woo, this is bad lightning!* I also remember sitting at the bar and seeing a big jar of something with dead worms in it. I asked the bartender what they were. "Pickled worms. They're considered a delicacy in a glass of tequila." He also told me that their tequila was especially delicious.

Needless to say, I didn't drink any tequila with pickled worms. Actually, I was still seventeen and didn't drink at all.

It was coke for me. But I did become more and more curious about what was going on upstairs. I kept seeing men going up the stairway with women, and then people coming down the stairs. Up the stairs...down the stairs...all night long. I finally asked the bartender what was going on. He calmly told me that a whorehouse was upstairs. "Oh, my *God*! If my grandparents only knew I was working in a whorehouse!" He told me that no one would bother me and to just ignore it. He was right, so that is what I did.

The people who told me not to drink the water and not to eat food that I didn't recognize were also right. But I got food poisoning anyway. I drank hot chocolate one night at the club that must have been made with local water. It was delicious but I paid dearly for it: I was *one sick puppy* – for several days. But Ross Valore took good care of me and I kept on working.

Every night I had to go back across the bridge to El Paso. I did this every night except for two. The first night I didn't go back, I had met a handsome, young Mexican boy. We were about the same age. The thing was, he didn't speak English and I didn't speak Spanish. But we were so attracted to each other that it didn't matter. We went to his small apartment and spent the night together. No talking, just sex — beautiful sex. We created a way for international communication all our own. And it was wonderful. It's too bad it can't solve the problems we have today. I could suggest it, though.

The second night I didn't cross the bridge to my hotel, I had met a handsome, debonair older man from Paris. He was so continental, the sex appeal just oozed. He owned a nightclub and restaurant in Juarez; the night after we met, he invited me over for a late dinner after my last show. He had closed the restaurant early and filled the dining room with roses and candles; the band was playing beautiful, romantic music, and he had this wonderful champagne that he kept pouring. He didn't know that I was seventeen and didn't drink anything. I got so drunk that he put me to bed in his office. After that, we saw each other every night until my contract ended. I later found out that he was married, so nothing came of that romance. But what a romantic adventure it was!

I had a very successful engagement in Juarez, but I also learned very good lessons: be careful that you are not booked in a whorehouse, don't drink the water, and be careful not to drink too much champagne because you will pass out. This is still simple and good advice.

When I returned from Juarez, I split my time between bookings at Louie's 29 Club and Jake Samara's Derby Club. One night when I was working at the Derby Club, comedian Victor Borge came in with his wife and manager. When they invited me to join them at their table at the end of my first show, I was very happy to do so. They told me how much they had enjoyed my performance and invited me to go downtown with them to have breakfast after my last show. So I went. What a lovely couple they were! And Mr. Borge was just a *lovely* man.

Mr. Borge's manager was nice, too. I can't recall his name. But I still remember the offer he made: he wanted to sign me to a contract to take me out of burlesque, bring me to New York City, and put me in legitimate Broadway shows. But stupid, young me turned him down. This may have been a mistake, but I think it was also the moment that I decided to stay in burlesque.

I met a lot of people when I worked at the Derby Club, and many of them became friends of mine. Back in those days in Oklahoma City, you had to carry a bottle of whiskey in a sack and you ordered set-ups in the nightclubs. I made friends with Dude and JD Wilson, two bootleg brothers that supplied whiskey to Jake Samara. I even dated JD for a little while. I also became friends with Russell Kofer—who was called the Bicycle Bootlegger because he had lost his driver's license.

I had known Russell's girlfriend, Peggy Sims, since I was a kid, living across a grasshopper-infested field from her parents' place on my grandparents' farm. It was Peggy who introduced me to Jack Johnson, the father of my only child. He was also the man who would turn my life upside-down and inside out. That story is next.

All burlesque stars were required to have head shots as part of their publicity packet. This was from my first shot at the age of 17, in 1952.

My second publicity photo at the age of 18.

Proof that I finally removed more than the gloves. I look "tough" here, but I really wasn't at all: I usually looked so innocent on stage.

Publicity photo from the Derby Club in 1956. I was 21.

Chapter Four

Love, Marriage, And Cyrese

By the time I met Jack Johnson, I was the star of the show at Louie's 29 Club in Oklahoma City. I was just eighteen and the critics loved me. They thought that I added innocence to the "sensual act of disrobing" or—in plain English—thought I was sexy as hell when I took off my clothes. While many burlesque stars had a gimmick (like a snake or a bathtub,) my gimmick was being who I was: innocent-looking and young. Being the star meant that you were headlined on the marquee; it meant that you were the last one on during the show. I was starting to make it and I loved it. I was where I belonged and never thought about being an actress or about where or what I would move on to. I wasn't interested in anything other than dancing—but I always did have an eye for a good-looking man. This was my strength and my big weakness.

I met Jack in Oklahoma City. We were introduced by one of my mother's friends, Peggy Simms, who was dating the Bicycle Bootlegger. At one time, Peggy lived across the field from us on one of our small farms. Mom was living with us between one of her marriages and became friendly with Peggy even though Peggy was more my age than hers. Peggy and I were friends, too, and I used to run like crazy across the field to see her. I would scream and jump all the way because grasshoppers would be jumping all over me. I hated them. Well, Peggy worked at the State Theatre in Oklahoma City and it was there that she met Jack, who was an usher. One night after my show she introduced us.

It was lust at first sight. He had a chiseled appearance, with dark hair, a dimple on one side, a great smile, and eyes that you could drown in. He was about 5'10", almost six-foot. Today, I would say that he looked like John Travolta when he was in *Urban Cowboy*. I was immediately attracted to his looks and his eyes: I drowned in them and didn't want to come up for air. Jack was still living at home with his parents who were devout Catholics: they had converted to Catholicism late in life and were really serious about it. I came from a Baptist family, but didn't go to church often. His parents didn't like that and liked less that I was in burlesque. They saw it as a sinful way of life and tried really hard to get Jack to stop seeing me.

After a few months, I realized that it was more than lust with Jack. It was his eyes, his smile and his ability to make me feel loved and cared for. And he made me laugh. Today, they would say that he was a keeper. I wasn't thinking that far ahead, but then I had to: I learned that I was pregnant. Jack was so sweet; after talking with him, we decided to get married (remember, he had strong religious beliefs.) We wound up getting married in a judge's chambers; one of my cousins who had looked me up in Oklahoma City was our witness. I wore the same beige suit as I did at my first wedding. It was a little sad because there was really no one there to celebrate with us and we were so casually dressed. And then, Jack almost immediately left for a new job.

When we got married, I was featured at Louie's 29 Club and Jack and his friend, Mike Kelly, had found jobs in Flint, Michigan at the Buick factory. The automobile factories paid good money. They soon left town and I finished my contract at Louie's 29. By then, I was starting to show, so I went and bought maternity clothes and flew to Flint. Jack and Mike had found an apartment; Mike was staying in the apartment too. In fact, when I got there, Mike *still* stayed in the apartment for a while. But Jack acted very loving, now that he was away from his mother. We were still very compatible and happy, even with Mike with us most of the time.

One day when I was at a new friend's baby shower, there was a tornado. We were across town and I got stuck there because I couldn't leave. The tornado was terrible. Outside the house where we were, cars were wrapped around trees and wires were down everywhere. I ended up stuck there for a couple of days. I was so stressed. I knew how worried Jack and my grandparents must have been. Once I finally got home, I slipped on a bathroom rug and fell. The fall and the stress caused early labor: I started bleeding and thought that I was going to lose the baby. Jack drove me to the hospital and the baby was born the next day, albeit a little early. I was so scared during the labor, but the baby was beautiful and healthy. We named our daughter Cyrese Lorraine and — to appease Jack's mother — we soon had her baptized in the Catholic Church. Before she was born, we had decided to move back to Oklahoma City. We thought it would be safer and closer to family. Mike decided that he would stay in Flint, so just the two of us moved. Back in Oklahoma, we lived for a while with my mother and her husband. My Jack was looking for a job and an apartment for us. I was happy with our family and loved Jack and Cyrese so much. I thought I was getting the "happily ever after" that I dreamed of and was willing to give up burlesque.

Just before Cyrese's first birthday, Jack finally found an apartment and made a big deal about showing it to me. My grandparents babysat for us. Oddly, he suggested that I go to the movies alone while he and his father finished setting up the apartment. I thought this was strange, but just went along with it. After the movie, they picked me up. I soon noticed that they were driving to a bad part of town; I said something and they ignored me. We pulled up in front of an old building, next to which was an empty lot filled with garbage. It was then that I had an uneasy feeling. When in the dingy apartment, he calmly told me that he was leaving Cyrese and me—and he just walked away and down the stairs. That was it. I was devastated. I followed him down the stairs, crying and pleading with him to stay. But he just kept walking. It was over.

I then realized that someone had moved all of Cyrese's and my things into the dirty apartment. I called my grandfather and he came and got us; we then moved in with them. I kept trying to call Jack, to visit or talk to him any way I could. He just refused. I knew his mother was behind it: she never accepted me and even thought that Cyrese wasn't Jack's. She never let that go; after being close to her again, he gave in.

I experienced despair and depression like never before and never again. This was truly the first major rejection of my life and I just couldn't cope. I had never expected all of the other short relationships to work, but I was in this one for the long haul and he wasn't. I had given up my identity and left burlesque; I'd gone back to being Velma and that wasn't good enough for him. I thought he left me as easily as my father left my mother and I was full of panic. I felt betrayed and abandoned and full of fear. I couldn't pull myself out of the darkness no matter what I did—and so I withdrew. I couldn't do anything, and after some time ended up having a nervous breakdown. I went to a doctor who gave me some pills. When I went home, I took some and went into the bathroom. I don't remember cutting my wrists with a razor blade, but I ended up in the hospital with a cast on my right arm. I had cut every tendon and artery in my right arm; to this day, I still have no feeling on one side of that hand. Jack knew about this but never came to see me. He didn't care and had really left us.

It took me a long time to recover physically and mentally. Benny, my first husband who I had treated so badly, came to see me every day and took me for long rides. He kept telling me that life goes on and that I had a beautiful daughter to care for. He became one of my dearest friends. He had remarried and had a child of his own, but he was there for me in a big way. After hearing this, I decided to divorce Jack. At the court appearance, his so-Catholic mother testified that she didn't think Cyrese was Jack's child. Still, he was ordered to pay child support. He never did pay, however, and I never took him back to court. I was left with the challenge of supporting Cyrese myself. The only time Jack came to see Cyrese was on her first birthday — and he didn't even bring her a present. He just came in and out and wouldn't talk to me.

My friend, Linda Powers, and her boyfriend, Jack Sussy, came to my rescue. Jack had an Italian restaurant where I took a job as a hostess. I only had to seat customers and give them a menu. This I could do with a cast on my arm. That job was a lifesaver after such an awful time and I will always be thankful to them for helping me out. For a while, I also taught ballroom dancing and there was this big, tall guy with a mustache named Bill that kept trying to make passes at me. He was way older than me, and I didn't like him that much. He had this crush on me and wanted to try to get me to go out with him but I wouldn't. And then he told me that he knew my ex-husband: he said that Jack was dating another woman named Ivenie. I said, "What do you mean, you know my ex-husband?" And he responded that he knew Jack and his girlfriend. Then he astounded me by saying that he had some interesting photos of them which he would show me if I stopped by his apartment. I know that it's awful that this piqued my curiosity, but it did. I went to his apartment and he brought out an envelope full of photos. They were all of Jack having sex with another woman.

I felt stupid because I was pining away for this man. I mean, I slashed my wrists because of Jack Johnson—and then I saw those pictures. I knew I had to move on. I got out of that man's apartment quickly because I realized that the situation was really creepy. As soon as the cast came off, back to burlesque I went. I started working again at Jake Samara's Derby Club, where I had once worked as a cigarette girl. I was back where it all started and back where I belonged. I was starting over. April March was back and life went on.

From that point, caring for Cyrese was my priority. At first, I only took bookings in Oklahoma City or in areas close by. In later years (when I could afford housekeepers and babysitters,) I again started to take out-of-town bookings. At different times, we had houses in Florida and New Jersey. I always sent Cyrese to Catholic schools to honor her father's faith. Once, she brought a picture of me to class to show her friends what her mother did. Needless to say, I quickly received a call from a properly shocked nun. More on this later.

Much later, years and years later, Jack's mother contacted me to apologize for what she did. I forgave her but it was way too late to make any difference in my life or in Jack's. Our marriage didn't work and we all had moved on.

Jack Johnson, with his pride and joy: his car: taken in Flint, Michigan in 1953.

My grandfather, Elmer Gragg, with Cyrese in Oklahoma City in late 1953.

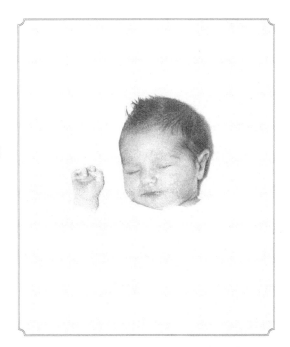

Cyrese at birth on July 19, 1953. She was so beautiful and immediately became the center of my universe.

Cyrese in 1957 with Santa in Oklahoma City.

One of Cyrese's school pictures. I think she was about 9 and we were living in Florida.

Chapter Five

My Men: Some I Married and Some I Didn't

W hile burlesque theatres were like fancy nightclubs, it is a fact that the intended audience was always men, especially the ones who came in by themselves without a date or their wife. We flirted with them outrageously, and in return they bought us drinks, gave us big tips, and sometimes bought us jewelry, furs, and clothes. If a romance developed, we might have slept with them. Yet most relationships were platonic: many of the girls were married and some (like me) even had children. After Jack, I really wasn't that interested in men, anyway. So I became a little more distant and a little more intriguing than I was before. Of course, this doesn't mean that I didn't marry two more men in the year following the divorce.

First, there was my gay hairdresser, Glen Quick. He begged me to marry him to convince his parents that he was heterosexual. Being gay was something to be ashamed of back then. At first, I said no. And then, I said no again. But then I realized that a good hairdresser is hard to find and gave in. We got married and went to visit his parents, who were thrilled. When we went back to Oklahoma City, we lived with Bill, his boyfriend. That was okay for a while, but there came a point when I wanted a more normal life for Cyrese and me. I divorced Glen and got an apartment for the two of us.

To supplement my income, I started to teach dance again at the local Xavier Cugat Studio. It was there that I met Fred Jhan, who was also an instructor. We started to date casually and soon he wanted to marry me. There was no love on my part and he knew it, but still he wanted to get married. I was just nineteen and felt that a husband would give me more security. Besides, I also thought that it would make Jack jealous. Even then, I think I still held onto some notion that he would come back to Cyrese and me if I just kept trying. This was just stupidity. After a few months, I wanted out of that marriage and Fred didn't really object. I think he thought that I would fall in love with him or at least in love with the marriage. By the time I left, he knew that it wasn't going to happen. This all means that by my twentieth birthday, I had been married four times — more than my mother's record.

During that time, there were some men that I didn't marry. Really! Bob Hanson, a burlesque comic with whom

I worked, became a friend—and we got along really well. When he asked me to marry him, I said yes: we were spending a lot of time together and had a lot of fun. But then I told him that I didn't love him and we split up. Right about that time, I met Dale Robertson: we went out a few times, but he was really full of himself. I stood him up one morning when I was supposed to meet him for breakfast, and never heard from him again. Shortly after that, I met Mel Torme, *the* Mel Torme! The owner of the club where I performed closed the burlesque show for two weeks and booked Mel Torme for a two-week engagement. One night, he invited me to meet Mel and we hit it off right away.

I always remember our first date with a smile. Mel was short: he told me to wear my hair down, to wear low heels, and that he hated red nail polish. He picked me up outside of Kerrs Department Store where I had had my hair done in an elaborate up-do and my nails painted red. I had such a pretty dress on with a swingy-type skirt and the highest heels you can imagine. He didn't mention anything about how I was dressed, and off we went to lunch and then to the movies. After that, we wanted to go to the drive-in to see a Western starring Rory Calhoun, who was a friend of his. I told him that he had a nine o'clock show; I didn't think we had time. He said that we had plenty of time and off we went. Well, we had a little tryst in the car and both fell soundly asleep. I woke at ten and told him that we had to hurry. Jake was so mad when we got back to the Derby Club: Mel was late for his first show and Jake had a club full of unhappy customers. He blamed it on me and told me to keep away from Mel. Of course, that wasn't going to happen.

I became infatuated with Mel and we got to know each other over the two weeks he was in Oklahoma City. When he left, I would either visit him or he would come back to town and spend time with me and Cyrese. He even met my entire family, which was unusual given that I didn't normally let men into my private world. When we couldn't see each other, we had a telephone romance which was a lot of fun. I guess I invented phone sex, something I am very proud of.

I still liked elaborate up-dos and high, high heels. It was silly but we would fight over this. We were so compatible, though: we would take long walks, go to the movies, and spend fun afternoons with Cyrese. It was so easy with him. A few months later, he asked me to marry him and I said yes without thinking or asking myself all of the important questions. After the wedding, Cyrese and I were supposed to go on tour with him; after that, we would live in Hollywood and he would continue his tours and music career. Almost as soon as I said yes, the thoughts started: I would have to give up burlesque; I would be sitting in Hollywood with nothing to do; I'd be Velma Fern again; Cyrese would be in the spotlight; all show business marriages end up in divorce. These ideas and more raced through my mind. Making matters worse, my mother and agent found a way into the story: they had met Mel, loved him, and thought I was crazy to even consider breaking up with him. I began to question whether or not I was really in love with him. I really hated those bow ties that he always wore: the ties were his trademark and I knew I couldn't change him.

It was then that I got booked into the Stardust in Tulsa, Oklahoma; Bob Hanson, too, was booked there and he and his wife, Sue, were staying at the same hotel. I used to always talk to them about how I wanted a normal life for Cyrese, a life away from burlesque. One night, a young, handsome gentleman was in the club and Bob Hanson said, "April, there's a friend of mine. He owns a few drugstores and he's single and a very nice person." He went on, "I'd like to introduce you." Well, I went over and met the man that was to be Husband #5. We dated a short while and then I married Charles Butler.

Common sense had taken over. I had a four year old daughter: I couldn't go on the road with her; I needed a normal life. I broke the engagement with Mel Torme over the telephone. Mel had called me from Pittsburgh, where we were supposed to meet. I said, "I can't come, I'm getting married to someone else." The old fears had won. I just knew that I couldn't live as a Hollywood wife, and Mel had met and fell in love with April March. How would he have reacted to Velma Fern? A "normal life" versus "show business" was always a struggle for me — and I didn't always make the right decision. Anyway, Mel got very mad and hung up the phone. After a few years, we did become phone buddies again and would call each other when we were down or depressed.

These conversations were not very uplifting. But I always respected Mel. Years later, I ran into him in Washington, D.C.: it was awkward at first, but then our affection for each other took over. I will always consider him one of my loves and best friends.

I left show business again, this time for six years. I became a member of two country clubs: the Indian Hills Country Club and Tulsa Country Club. I took up golf and became the Vice President of the Women's Golf Association. I loved golf and was quite good at it, I didn't let anyone know that I was April March; I only used my real name. Charles just wanted me to be Mrs. Butler, not a burlesque star with a past. But there were a few of the members (men) that said, "You look so familiar." I'm sure that they had seen me perform at one time or another. But I would just coyly say, "Oh, you must be mistaken. I don't know where you could have met me."

I lived the suburban, country club life with my daughter and Charles. I had maids and I had…well, I had everything I wanted. I lived a very good life. We had frequent vacations in Florida—but I was still not content. I was really bored. I missed show business and again felt that restlessness. I wanted to be on that stage. I wanted applause. I wanted to be performing. I wanted to be traveling. I wanted burlesque. I didn't really want Charles.

To placate me, Charles sold the drugstores and Charles, Cyrese and I moved to Miramar, Florida, just north of Miami Beach. It was one of the places that Charles and I liked to go on vacation. We went out every day, playing golf. But I got bored with that, too. I told Charles that I wanted to go back to burlesque, and he *really* didn't like the idea. He was quite jealous: he said that he just didn't like the idea of men looking at my body. But I was adamant: I told him that I was going back into burlesque. There really wasn't anything more he could say or do.

I found a costume-maker and had a few gowns made; I found an agent in Miami, Roland Muse, and he booked me into the beautiful Clover Club. I went in there and worked seven nights a week. I didn't mind, because there I was back on that stage again...I loved the applause that I got. I don't know why, but all my life I have seemed to require and want that attention. By that time, Charles and I had been married for pretty close to six years. But we just couldn't make a go of it: he couldn't handle me being in burlesque and I couldn't be the stay-at-home wife that he wanted. I had also cheated on him by going on a date with the bartender from the Clover Club, and afterward made sure that he found out about it. He was waiting for me that night and when I got home we made quite a scene. After, he became quiet and told me that the marriage was over. He was calm and civilized: he just moved out of the house and made arrangements to move back to Tulsa. I was sorry that I was so awful to Charles, but there was no way I could have been who he wanted.

Not long after Charles left, I was working at the Clover Club in Miami and getting used to being alone again, supporting

Cyrese and myself. One night, a wealthy and very attractive couple came in and asked me to join them for a drink. After some routine polite conversation, the very proper-looking wife said that they would pay me $10,000 to come back to their hotel and let them bathe me in champagne. They assured me that there would be no sex, only champagne in the tub in their suite. For that amount of money, I thought why not? They stopped along the way and bought three cases of Piper Heidspeck Brut, put it in the cab, and back to the Fontainebleau Hotel we went. Believe me — that bath was cold and tingly. The bathroom was big and beautiful with a window overlooking Miami Beach. They had lit candles and used big colorful sponges to slowly and methodically stroke my body. They were looking at each other and casually chatting. After getting out of the tub, I got dressed and they handed me $10,000 in cash. They then walked me to the lobby, put me in a cab, and we said goodbye. I never saw them again. It was the easiest $10,000 I had ever made and the strangest. Even then, my life was never dull.

Shortly after this, I met Lili St. Cyr. She had come in as the star of the show, and I was reduced to co-star status. Lili became the reigning lady of burlesque in the 1940s and 1950s, after Gypsy Rose Lee and Ann Corio retired. I was not happy about the co-star status, but when I met Lili, we became friends — and she really did not like most people. She wouldn't even let *anyone* in her dressing room. But one night, I couldn't find my white gloves and needed gloves for my act. When her husband heard this, he went and told her and she gave her husband a pair of *her* white gloves to bring to the dressing room for me. After using them, I took them home, washed and ironed them, and returned them the following evening. And that's when she invited me into the dressing room for a cup of tea. I found out that she was a very shy, lovely, and complicated lady. Even though she was almost twenty years older than me, we became friends. We had a lot in common: we had both been raised by our grandparents and had taken formal dance lessons that we used as the basis of our first acts. Also, we had both been married more than once. Sometime later, she wanted to sell me her bathtub act, the cornerstone of her performances. I really wanted to buy it, but Sam Shanker, the owner of the Clover Club, talked me out of it. He said that I wasn't making that kind of money, and that it would be too costly for me to take that tub on the road; he said that I would have to hire a maid to go with it — to do the act with me (Lili had a maid wrap a towel around her when she stepped out of the bathtub naked.) He talked me out of it, and I reluctantly let him do it. I always regretted not buying that act and incorporating it into my performances. It's an act that I would have loved to have done; I think I would have been good at it. Mostly, though, it would have been a permanent tie between Lili and me.

I stayed in Miami for quite some time. I got a divorce from Charles and he went back to Oklahoma while I remained in Florida. Before he left, he hired a housekeeper to take care of Cyrese while I worked. He really was a wonderful man; I was very sad that I couldn't be the woman that he wanted. At about this time, I met Prince Mansour and Prince Thamir of Saudi Arabia. I had opened in a club called The Picadilly in Miami Beach for Sam Shanker. I was starring there when he booked Blaze Starr. Again, my billing was reduced to co-star, with Blaze Starr as the headliner. Well, I wasn't too happy about it this time — once was really enough. Blaze had gained national notoriety because of her affair with Governor Huey Long of Louisiana and was the subject of a biopic, "Blaze," starring Paul Newman as the Governor. Later on, she claimed to have had an affair with President Kennedy, but I think everyone who casually met him claimed the same. Anyway, in the late 1950s, she was the headliner wherever she worked.

One night, two princes from Saudi Arabia came in with nineteen aides and bodyguards. They saw the show, and I was the only one that they invited to their table. They didn't want Blaze; they wanted April. I still chuckle about this. So I went. The two princes were well-educated and spoke English well. I was invited to go to lunch with them the following day in Palm Beach. I was thrilled. They said that they would send a limousine to pick me up. They found out where I lived, and sure enough, the next day, the limousine came (along with two bodyguards to watch out for me) and I was whisked off to Palm Beach. I had a delightful afternoon with the two of them. We played checkers, drank and sat in the sun, and talked. They weren't supposed to smoke because they were Muslim, but they did. Prince Thamir gave me a wooden cigarette case that I still have. They asked me for autographed photos, which I knew that they wanted and had them with me, one for each of them. When we said goodbye, I was put in the limousine and whisked back to Miami Beach where I was performing that night. Well, Blaze was *very* unhappy that I was getting all this attention—that I had gone to Palm Beach as the guest of King Saud's two favorite sons. I think he had something like one hundred and twenty-five children, but he had favorites: among the sons, Prince Mansour and Prince Thamer were favorites. They were the two that he brought with him from Saudi Arabia. He had come to America for an eye operation in Boston, but what nobody knew was that he also had an appendectomy there. The King wouldn't stay in Miami Beach because of the high number of Jewish residents. He asked to meet me, though, when he saw the photos that I left with the princes. Thus, my mata-hari story began.

A couple of days went by before I got a call at the club from a gentleman that said that he worked for the government—our government. He introduced himself as Frank Mulhaus. He asked if he could meet with me the following afternoon. Of course, I said yes. He had set up a place for a meeting: he told me that our government had been trying to get a letter to the King of Saudi Arabia, and that no one could get this letter through. It was supposedly a very, *very* important letter. Frank Mulhaus knew that I was going to meet the King, and so my adventure into spying began. Again, a limousine and bodyguards picked me up: I went to Palm Beach with the letter tucked inside my bra.

I met the King. There must have been 25 bodyguards and aides there. Frank Mulhaus had warned me: "Don't drink or eat *anything* when you go to the mansion." The King had taken over a millionaire's mansion while in Palm Beach, and he had taken over four other houses for the four wives he brought with him. A man by the name of Becca Eunice was his personal representative and a man by the name of Abraham was the ambassador to Saudi Arabia. Abraham wasn't very polite to me: he gave me dirty looks all the time and obviously did not want to be involved in the letter transfer. Anyway, Frank Malhaus had given me the words in Arabic that meant "letter from Frank Malhaus." He had instructed me until I remembered what to say. I still remember the orange chiffon dress that I wore and the short sweater with the fur collar. The dress swirled around my legs when I walked. When I got to the mansion, my press agent, who was Jewish, was told to stay in the limousine. I went in alone and had quite a lengthy wait. Finally, Becca Eunice came in and showed me how to curtsy properly: he said I had to curtsy when the King came into the room and that I was not to sit before the King sat. He was going to interpret, since the King spoke only Arabic and I spoke only English.

The room was elegantly furnished. The King came into the room and all went silent. He was dressed in Saudi robes that flowed around him as he walked. The first thing I noticed was how large his feet were in the brown leather sandals he was wearing. His appearance was just so impressive. When the King was standing in front of me, I politely curtsied as I was taught. I was so nervous that I then sat down (really, fell down) on the sofa behind me. I was sweating so profusely that the letter was getting wet. And oh, I was so nervous! My throat was so dry I couldn't talk and I had been told not to drink anything. Sitting down caused a lot of chaos. Everyone was gasping and making strange faces. Everyone knew that I sat down before the King!

But he patted my head and let me know it was all right. When we were talking he asked me where I was from; I said, "Oklahoma City, Oklahoma." I told him that I was English, Irish, and Cherokee Indian. He was quite intrigued by my ancestry, showing particular interest in my Native American ancestors. He then said, "You are such a beautiful girl." And, right away, he said, "I want to invite you to come home with me." He said, "I'm going to my castle in Majorca and then I'll be going to the castle in Saudi Arabia—the palace, my home." And he said, "I want you with me." Meanwhile, I'm thinking, "Oh! Oh! My *goodness*! This man moves fast." I could tell that he was used to getting what he wanted. Then I thought of the publicity I would get with such a trip! Finally, I remembered the letter and said the words in Arabic that I was taught. He understood what I said and I told Becca Eunice that I had to give him this letter in private.

We went into the King's chambers. It was a room right out of Arabian nights—sheer curtains and candles all over. It was so romantic. We "spoke" for a while and then I took out the letter; the King read the letter and oh my *goodness*! He started ranting and raving. He called in Becca Eunice and they were talking in Arabic. He was *angry*, and I said, "Oh my *God*, what was in that letter?" I never did find out; I do know, however, that it was quite the way to destroy a mood. I was excused, but before I left the King asked me what I would like to have. He suggested some gold coins, and I joked that I wanted his signet ring—the ring that he used to put seals on official documents. He smiled coyly and said that he couldn't give me that but would give me anything else that I wanted. I said, "Well, I've always wanted a full-length white ermine coat." So the King (and Becca Eunice, who was interpreting) said that I would get the things that I wanted—but he wanted my answer about going away with the King the following day. He wanted to leave for home in a day or two. They then very nicely asked me to leave right then. At that moment, I fully intended to leave the country with him and I think he knew it.

The following day, I received a call from Becca Eunice: he asked, "Are you packed and ready to go?" In the meantime, Frank Malhaus called me and told me not to go because the government couldn't protect me. They also didn't want to do anything to anger the King, since the United States needed to continue using an airstrip in Saudi Arabia; they couldn't risk not being able to use that airstrip. Anyway, I saw all the publicity going down the drain. Something *wonderful* could have happened: all that money—*big, big* money—I could have made by being the girlfriend of a King, and I couldn't go because it wasn't safe to do so. I was very upset. But later on, I found out that Abraham had been beheaded, and then that the two sons, Prince Mansour and Prince Thamir, had both been assassinated. For a while, I corresponded with Frank Malhaus. I got several letters from him, thanking me and saying that everybody thought it was wonderful that I got the letter through to the King. He said that I made the right decision to not go to Majorca and Saudi Arabia. I never saw Frank again. I kept the letters for a while, but then through all of my moving, I lost them.

After this, I met a wonderful man named Manny Rabin. He and his brothers ran Westbury Fashions in New York City; he was vacationing in Florida. He looked like a young Paul Newman—he was so handsome. He came into the club one night and then every night while he was in the area. He courted me in an old-fashioned way. We sat on the beach and watched sunrises and sunsets. We went for breakfast and dinner and spent time with Cyrese. He gave me flowers and candy. When he got back to New York, he called me— sometimes three or four times a day—and sent me beautiful gifts. For example, he sent me a beautiful bracelet from Tiffany's, and a beautiful gold cigarette lighter. We continued our relationship via phone and mail, but once a week he would also fly in to see me. Then, all of a sudden, he said that he was going to be in Hagerstown, Maryland for business. He asked if I would like to go and meet him. I said yes.

At that time, I was still working in Miami Beach, so I made arrangements for Cyrese and took his private plane to Hagerstown. I got off the plane and into a limousine, where we headed to the hotel. The driver of the limo said that Mr. Rabin was at the plant, but that I should go in and get unpacked. He also asked that I unpack Manny's suitcase while I was at it. He said that Mr. Rabin would be there as soon as possible and that then we'd go out for dinner.

So, that's just what I did: I went in and got unpacked, and then began to unpack his suitcase. As I was unpacking his suitcase, though, I found a prescription in there that was written out to a "Helene Rabin." It was for prenatal capsules of some kind. I thought, "Helene. Helene, Helene." I thought, "Oh, my God. Who in the world could that be?" When he finally got to the hotel and walked through the door, I was sitting there holding that prescription and he looked at me. And he looked, and his face turned white. I said, "Manny, who is Helene Rabin?" And he said, "Oh my God, April. You found out...*Please* don't leave me. *Please* don't leave me." He said, "I am married."

I said, "You're *married*?? What is this, for prenatal?"

Calmly, he said, "My wife is pregnant and I have two older children."

I said, "Oh my *God*, Manny, How could you *do* this?"

I was so upset because I was madly in love with him. He started crying; he said, "I *can't* lose you. I *can't* lose you."

He was an Orthodox Jew. I knew what a torment this was; he was a tormented person. He was in love with me, but he was Orthodox. He wouldn't or couldn't leave his wife and I knew it from that point on. I didn't know *what* to do. He kept saying that he couldn't lose me.

As for our relationship, I mean—we had had such a *beautiful* relationship. We had gone to Boston. We had gone to so many places. We just had a beautiful romance, and I loved him dearly. I didn't know what to do: I told him that I wanted his plane, his pilot, to take me back to Miami right away. I said, "We've got to think things over." And then I said, "I can't believe you started our relationship with this lie." I went back to Miami and buried myself with work and with taking care of Cyrese.

Soon after, I was involved in a horrible shooting incident at The Pigalle. Just before, I had met the lawyer of a deposed dictator who had settled in Miami under the protection of our government. He invited me to go on a yacht to the Bahamas with him. By that time, I had developed gout in my foot and really wasn't well—I was on crutches and stressed out. Yet I went on the yacht anyway, and took a short cruise to the Bahamas with the lawyer. I had a good time, but was thinking about the problems I had and about Manny, thinking and wondering what to do.

Following the Bahamas trip, I went back to Miami. It was here that my lawyer friend told me that he was proficient in belly dancing, too! Imagine: a lawyer who could teach belly dancing! Years before, he had taught Broadway dancer Nejla Ates how to belly dance. Since The Pigalle had banned stripping when they reopened, I learned an authentic belly dance from this lawyer/teacher so that I could go on as a belly dancer. Regardless, I got arrested the first night even though I didn't take anything off. The police were really gunning for burlesque dancers then. I was doing an authentic belly dance when this detective, Mickey, arrested me for "lewd and lascivious performance." I spent the night in jail, and the following day—here I was, still in the belly dance costume—I was given a summons to appear in court. I had called the attorney for the club, The Place Pigalle, to prepare my release: when I left the police station, photographers waited on the steps as I passed by in my costume and with the summons in-hand. Well, *that* made magazines all over the world, not to mention the newspaper.

When I finally went to court, the lawyer directed me to remove my coat in front of the judge. When I took off the coat, the judge asked, "This is how you were dressed?"

"Yes, sir," I said.

The judge pounded the gavel. "Case dismissed." With that, I was exonerated. I really got a lot of publicity from the whole thing: the detective even got fired. But then, *True Detective* wrote this *wild* story that called me a "femme fatale:"

I could have sued the magazine, but the lawyer told me not to. He thought that it would just cause more harassment and a lot of grief; he said that I should just let it go. "It's publicity, anyway. Even though it makes you infamous," he said. "It's still publicity."

At that point, I started thinking of all the awful things that had happened in Miami. I was even robbed at a motel: a lot of furs and jewels were stolen. I just thought *I've got to get out of Miami Beach for a while*. My daughter, of course, was there and in school: she would need to stay. So I made plans for Cyrese to stay with the parents of one of her friends and I sold my home in Miramar. I went off to find myself — though I was still seeing Manny, off and on, despite not knowing what would happen there. I was so much in love with him that I didn't want to break everything off. Yet I felt *terrible*. I knew what a turmoil *he* was in, too.

Well, I went on the circuit. I went to Boston and signed a contract with Jess Mack to work the B&E Circuit (named for the owners, Frank Bryan and Frank Engle.) I figured that it would be a *lot* better for me to work theatres, where I wouldn't come in contact with the audience. I considered all the bad things that had happened lately; I thought this would be a welcome change. So I started working the theatre circuit — the specifics of which I'll go into later, but not in a chapter about romance!

I signed a contract with Jesse Mack in Boston. It was then and there that I met Frank Engle, one of the owners of the

B&E circuit. He was getting over a big romance with Tempest Storm; he didn't show up in all of the theatres like he used to when he was dating Tempest. On the day I signed the contract, he took one look at me and said, "Hey, Kiddo! You wanna go for a blintz?" Now, I had never eaten a blintz before. When I told him, he said that I was in for a big treat and off we went. He knew this wonderful deli in Boston: he said, "we're gonna go and get you a blintz, Kiddo." From then on, that was his nickname for me. We went and got the blintz and sat and talked for a long time. He was very easy to talk to. I got along well with him, and he told me that I was going to be a wonderful addition to his theatres. So I told him that I thought I was going to very happy working for him and I told him about all the things that had happened recently.

I started in working the theatres. Manny would fly in, no matter where I happened to be: if I was in Cleveland, he would fly in and stay overnight in Cleveland; if I was in St Louis, there he would be. He would still tell me that he didn't know what to do, but also that he still couldn't leave Helene. He was making himself and me sick. I was so afraid that he was going to have a nervous breakdown.

One of the engagements for Frank Engle was in Toronto, Canada at the Casino Theatre. The ensemble was staying at a very nice hotel, The Westbury. Frank was pursuing me by this time and Manny and he were fighting for my attention. They would both fly in for opening nights and send flowers for my dressing room. Well, this one night I was having dinner with Frank and one of the waiters told me Manny was waiting for me in my room upstairs. I kept going back and forth trying to keep them both happy. Manny figured out what was going on and got so mad he put his fist through the wall in my room. Yet, he was the one that was still married.

I decided that I had to get out of that situation. I needed to do something drastic: I asked Jesse Mack if he could book me any place overseas for a few months. He suggested that I go work in Manchester, England: he told me that there was a booking; I would be the next star at the Arthur Fox Revue Bar for three months. I told him that I had heard awful things about working in England and that the climate was supposed to be dreary, but it was the only suggestion he had. I figured, *well, maybe this will give Manny a chance to decide what he wants to do, what he* has *to do.* Sadly, I knew what he had to do—he just wouldn't accept it. So I took the booking. I reluctantly left Cyrese, but knew that I had to get away. She was in good hands in Florida, and she was in school; I couldn't take her anyway.

Manny put me on the plane at Kennedy Airport to Manchester, England. We both cried. He said he was going to miss me, and he said that he wasn't going to be with me for my birthday because I was opening in May and my birthday was in June. I went to England and opened the Arthur Fox Revue Bar. I was *miserable.* It rained every day. It was damp, chilly and cold. I had no friends; I was by myself all the time. I discovered that I really didn't want that much time for soul searching. I lived in an old English boarding house in a small room with very little heat. I got used to being cold all the time. The land lady was lovely and very friendly; she became the closest thing I had to a friend. No matter what, though, I just wanted to go home.

And, of course, there was Mr. Fox. He took my passport "for safekeeping." He was just afraid I would run away on Sundays—my day off— and not return. He was afraid I'd get stuck in Paris or Italy or wherever I might go on a Sunday. He started sending a car to pick me up at the flat, every Sunday, to go over to his house for dinner. He was in mourning for his wife. We were just friends and had some lovely times. I continued to be so lonesome for my family. At the time, you had to book calls over to the United States: Manny would call me, and I called him once or twice. I called my daughter frequently. After that, I was *so* miserable and wanted to go home *so* badly that I turned down a contract to work six months throughout Europe, South Africa, and Japan. All I wanted to do was to just go home. The *News of the World* came over to do a big story on me, and doggone, the week that my story was supposed to be on the front page of the *News of the World*, the John Profumo scandal—the call girl scandal—broke out. As John Profumo was a big political figure over there, I thought, "Oh my *God*! What can happen next?" I said to myself, "I just want to go back to the States." So I did not take the bookings in Paris, or Italy, or any of those places that I would have liked to visit. I should have taken the bookings, but I missed Cyrese so much—I felt that I wanted and needed to be with her. I also had to resolve the Manny issue once and for all. I just missed being in my own country.

So, back home I came. Manny waited at the airport; it took a long time to go through customs back then. After we got my luggage and got into the car, he asked, "What would you like to do?" Quickly, I said, "I want to go to Coney Island. I want a potato niche, a Nathan's hot dog, and I want to ride the roller coaster." So that's where we went. We went to Coney Island. That night, he stayed with me and it was wonderful; we were just madly in love. The separation— the three-month, five day separation— it just didn't work. It didn't solve a thing. We were still madly in love, and he was still torn about what to do. His brothers were very upset because they had raised him; Manny's parents had died when he was very young and his three brothers were in business together. The other two liked me, but they told Manny that he couldn't leave his wife. They told him that he should always remember his religious beliefs which meant that he had to stay with Helene. It was such a big mess. Nothing was resolved. I told Manny that it was over and went back to my daughter in Florida, where I had all intention of staying.

Manny never really gave up on me until I married again, but after I left New York our affair was over. I had heard that he had two nervous breakdowns and was hospitalized after I left him. I saw him once more years later when I was working in the Silver Slipper in Washington, D.C. This was shortly before I retired. He was seated and sent me a note asking if I would come out and visit with him. When I saw the note, I turned pale and started shaking. I went out and talked with him. He was still so bitter and very unhappy. I did think about how everything had gone so wrong: I thought I was sending him back to his family. In fact he was still with Helene and he admitted that he would never leave her. He was the unhappiest person I had ever seen. He told me point-blank that I had destroyed his life and that he would never forgive me. With that, he walked out of the club and my life forever. I never heard from him or saw him again. It was such a sad story.

After I stopped seeing Manny, I went back to my daughter and stayed in Florida. I wanted some time off and some time alone with Cyrese. When we were together again, Cyrese told me about this nice policeman, Officer Marion, who had seen her riding her bicycle around. She told me that he kept checking on her to make sure she was alright. Cyrese finally introduced me to her new friend one afternoon when we were out riding our bikes together. The Officer drove up in his patrol car, and I met Joe Marion. Joe seemed to be really fond of my daughter and seemed like a nice guy. When he asked me out, I thought: *well at least he's single and he's a cop.* We went out on a few dates and met for drinks a few nights and inevitably wound up in bed. He was divorced and seemed to be very attentive to my needs. He was a good sex partner, but I didn't see that anything would come of the relationship.

I decided then that I had to get back to work. I needed money to support us. My agent booked me at the Club Copa in Cape Canaveral. When I was ready to leave, Joe said that he would drive me. By that time, I again had hired the housekeeper who had taken care of Cyrese when she was younger: I was renting a nice place, and I arranged for the housekeeper to take care of Cyrese. Joe came to Cape Canaveral with me and I opened at the club. I had brought a lot of jewelry and gifts from Manny with me. I thought that I was the only one that knew where everything was packed, but it turned out that Joe had watched me pack. To make a long story short, one day I went to get the bracelet and lighter—all this stuff—and realized that it was no longer in the suitcase. I asked Joe about it: he said, *oh*, he didn't know anything about it, and *it must have been the maid*. But I didn't have a maid: I had rented a small cottage and didn't need one. He *had* to have taken it, but I didn't want to think about that since he had been so nice to Cyrese and me.

Now, by that time I had decided to go back on the theatre circuit. An agent in Boston had contacted me, wanting to know if I was ready to go out again. I told Jesse Mack, "Okay. I'm ready." Well, Joe Marion spoke up and asked me if he could go with me, and I agreed. Instead of flying, Joe packed up and off we went in his white Cadillac, off to my new bookings. I later found out that the car had been given to him by an older woman who he was seeing before me.

He went with me to all of the theatres. Still, Manny was calling, crying all the time. Finally, when I was working a theatre in Youngstown, Ohio, Joe asked me to marry him: he said that it would stop all the nonsense. I thought to myself, if I get married, Manny will stop tormenting me—and he'll stay with Helene and his family. So as much as I loved Manny, I agreed to marry Joe. We went to Sharon, Pennsylvania and got married. Again, it was a quick justice of the peace affair. I didn't know then what a mistake it was to marry that man. I didn't know that his first wife ended up having a nervous breakdown after living with him, and he had done something *so terrible* in Trenton, NJ that he had to leave the City—ending up in Florida. Although he had somehow managed to get on the police force, I still think that he's the one who robbed me of Manny's gifts in Cape Canaveral. He wound up doing such awful things: he drank and he spent almost all of my money, going out with other women, buying them roses, wining and dining them, and telling them that he was single. But I didn't know about any of it for *years*.

He started hitting me occasionally, too. I would keep taking him back and I don't know why. A long time later (after we divorced,) I learned that he just did despicable things with my daughter, too.

I wound up getting an offer to star in the Minsky show: I was working the Charles Steakhouse in Hartford, Connecticut when I got a call to go to New York City to audition for Harold Minsky. Well, to be in a Minsky show is the epitome of burlesque. To me, the Minsky show was like a Ziegfeld Follies. It was the dream of every burlesque star: I mean, Gypsy Rose Lee starred with the Minsky shows! I was just so overjoyed. I flew from Hartford into New York City and met my agent Eddie Kaplan. At the meeting with Eddie, in walked Harold Minsky. He was a very good-looking, gray-headed, pipe-smoking gentleman; he said, "Miss March?" and I said, "Mr. Minsky?" We stood and talked for a few minutes. I said, "Do you want me to audition? I brought a costume." He said, "Miss March, you don't have to do any audition for me. You're hired. You're going to be the star of my next show."

Eddie immediately spoke up: "You already have that show booked."

"It doesn't matter," he said. "Miss March is going in as the star. The other girl will go on before Miss March." So I signed a contract as a star of the Minsky show in Yonkers, NY. I think the place was called the Westchester Town House.

By then, I was thinking: *How am I going to get out of this marriage?* I was having *so* much trouble with him. He was spending my money like crazy. I knew it, and then he'd drink, and then he'd slap me around. I thought, *how in the world can I take him to Yonkers?* Somehow, he wound up going to Yonkers. I kept trying to leave him and he just kept showing up as my husband. I kept asking for a divorce and he kept saying no. He had a good thing going and had no intention of letting it go.

I didn't find out about many of the things he did until later years. My daughter never said anything. No one ever said anything to me. In Yonkers, I stayed at the hotel where the show was located. In the mornings, I would go down to the coffee shop and then go back there later in the afternoon. I met all these gentlemen that were backstage every night at the show: they were always there and were so nice to me. Well, it turned out that they were mafia. But they were wonderful, wonderful gentlemen, and you would never have guessed what they really did. They were all quite respected business people in the community and so nice to me.

Harold Minsky developed a crush on me. He watched my show every night and waited for me afterwards. He bought stockings for me because he liked me to wear sheer stockings with a black stripe up the back. I was used to wearing just plain, sheer hose that were cheaper. He would do that, and he would buy me chocolates, and he would wait for me, we'd go into the bar and have a cup of coffee in-between shows and talk. It began to get a little serious, because he started to talk about future shows and about me going back to Vegas with him. Of course, there was Joe Marion to whom I was still married. I really had to do something about *him*.

One night after the show, I came off the stage and Joe was there and *spit* at me. My friends who I played gin rummy with at the coffee shop were there, too, and one picked him up by one elbow, and the other by the other elbow, and they dragged him out of the hotel. It was a comical sight—the stunned look on his face, the way they carried him like a sack of beans. When they came back in, they said that they gave him fifteen minutes to go to the room, pack his things, and get out of New York and go back to New Jersey. They said, "April, do you want us to do something to take care of this? He'll never bother you again and they'll never trace anything to you."

I said, "No, no, no. Just let him go back to Jersey."

"He can never come back here. While you're here, he can never come back. He can never step foot in here again."

"Fine," I said. I didn't see Joe, and the following day his mother called me from Trenton. She said that he was begging to come back. I said, "He can't come back here." And I said to her, "He's mistreating me. He's just terrible."

She said, "Oh, please give my son another chance." She never told me the truth about the things he had done before this. She didn't care about Cyrese or me: she just wanted me to take him back.

In the meantime, Minsky wanted me to do another show in Wildwood, NJ at the Manor Hotel. The people that owned the Manor Hotel caught the show in Yonkers and didn't want the other girl on the show. They said that they would take the show as long as I was still the star. So Minsky asked, "Will you go to Wildwood to the Manor? It's for ten weeks." I said yes. Quite happy, he said, "Well, from there, you can come back to Vegas with me. And then we'll put together another show designed just for you." I said, "We'll see what happens."

Everyone had convinced me to take Joe back again. Mind you, I didn't know all of the things that were going on, all the horrible things that he was doing—even my daughter never said anything. My daughter was ten years old at that time: he had scared her and kept warning her not to tell me anything. His parents also never told me anything. This went on for quite a few years. Anyway, he went to Wildwood with me, but he didn't go to the club or hotel much. I had a very successful ten-week engagement. Shortly after, I divorced Joe after over ten years of marriage and we went our separate ways. I thought he was finally out of my life for good. But you can never get rid of the bad memories created by men like him.

Just a little later, I was working for Sam Shanker at the Silver Slipper nightclub in Washington, D.C. Professor Irwin Corey was also on the show: he was the man that played the mad bomber in the movie *Car Wash*. We became good friends and stayed in the same hotel, with the Shankers paying for both of our rooms. Anyway, after *he* left the Silver Slipper, they brought in Joey Ross, Jr. and his sister, Alverda Ross. They did a comedy and pantomime act called Ross and Ross. That's how I met Joey—Lenny Ross, Jr. (his name was Lenny, but everybody called him Joey.) Anyway, we met and became fast friends. Between work and hanging out together, we were together pretty much all of the time. Joey and Alverda did a very good act, and they went over very well with the audiences. I then heard that they had a group called the Quaker City Follies. It was a variety show for which they did their comedy act and the pantomime routine. They had a belly dancer and a straight man, Ned (I don't remember Ned's last name.) Their niece, Michele, did the belly dance. There was also a girl who Joey dated for quite some time, a stripper on the show named Carol Ann. Anyway, I continued seeing Joey: I had just gotten over the divorce with Joe Marion, and I was in a pretty vulnerable state. After just a short time, I married him — Lenny Ross, Jr. We were both thirty-nine when we married. Both of us were Geminis, both born in June. I became the star of the Quaker City Follies show. Through my marriage to Joey, the Follies started to receive more and more work in better places: we even worked the Golden Banana in Peabody, Massachusetts. I was happy about working with the Quaker City Follies: Joey and I were more friends and business partners than anything else. The marriage only lasted a short time, perhaps less than two years, but we remained good friends. It was a good time in my life. There was not much drama and we were both pretty content.

Here, we need to go back a little bit to when I first met a man named Karl Ullman. It seems like I could never stay out of Washington, D.C. When Sam Shanker closed his clubs in Miami and Miami Beach, he moved back to Washington, D.C. and started opening nightclubs there instead. Sam kept calling me back to work at different clubs that were opening in the D.C. area. Once, I opened a club that he called The Celebrity Room where I met Karl Ullman, the Secretary/

Treasurer of the Teamsters' Union for the West Coast. I met Karl when he and his friend, John Sheridan (another teamster) came into the club. Between shows, he asked the waitress if he could meet me. The waitress told me that there were two very lovely gentlemen that wanted to meet me, and asked if I would go out and have a drink with them. I got into a long conversation with them and – I don't know – there just seemed to be an immediate attraction between Karl and me. We just talked and talked and talked. He and John stayed until The Celebrity Room closed and I did my last show. After, we decided to go out and have a bite to eat. I said, "You know, I'm hungry for White Castle hamburgers." So we went to a White Castle, got a bag of hamburgers, and the three of us went back to their hotel. We ordered room service for champagne. We ate White Castle hamburgers, drank champagne, and played gin rummy. Well, we played gin rummy until eight or nine o'clock in the morning when we went downstairs and had breakfast. Then, they had meetings to go to and I had to go to bed because I had a show that night. Anyway, for the three or four days that the Teamsters were in Washington, D.C., Karl came into the club every night. We developed a very good friendship and a wonderful, wonderful personal relationship that would last for years. In no time, we fell very much in love: it just felt so right. I was married to Joe Marion at the time, of course, and he was married to his wife, Barbara and had three grown children. After we met, we corresponded all the time and he called me frequently. He sent me flowers with love notes: they were so loving and caring. We just had the beginnings of a beautiful love affair; we were like magnets drawn to each other. Our lovemaking was so tender and so gentle that we just had to be together. Little did I know that he was to be the most important love of my life.

After we met, it seemed like every time I worked Washington, D.C. the Teamsters would be there for some meeting. After The Celebrity Club, I opened up a club right near there, for Sam Shanker, called the Paper Doll. And from the Paper Doll, I went back to The Celebrity Club, the Paper Doll, and the Silver Slipper. Later on, he would open up the Plaza Theatre. I just kept going back. In-between my theatre engagements on the road and those on the B&E circuit, I would wind up in Washington, D.C. And, of course, Karl would come to Washington, D.C. a lot to lobby the government. For thirteen years, we kept this beautiful romance going. Since we were married to other people, nothing more could come out of it—until, all of a sudden, I divorced Joe Marion. Karl was very happy about it, but Karl had been with his wife, Barbara, for so many years, and she was in the first stages of a battle with cancer. I saw no future and yet I was madly in love with Karl. I had thought that Manny Rabin had been my big love: but then, there was Karl. Yet again, I saw no future in that relationship either, and that's why I married Joey.

Karl still came to Washington frequently after Joey and I started working as a team. Joey had had an argument with his sister, Alverda, so I was doing the pantomime act plus the Burlesque Show. We were working a club called Fredrick's in Washington, D.C. and I opened up a club up above Fredrick's that he called "April's." I did that for several months, but in that time period Karl came back to D.C. and came to April's. And he drank a lot. *I* drank a lot. I missed a show because I was sitting with him; we were crying together about our lives. He liked Joey, but by then Joey knew that Karl was the big love of my life. After the show one night, we all even went out to breakfast together. Everybody — all the show people — used to go to a restaurant, an Italian restaurant, called Anna Maria's: it was the local hangout for all the performers in town. So Karl would take us to breakfast, and then we would drop Karl off at the hotel. Even though I was married, I would continue to correspond with and meet Karl whenever I could.

After the marriage with Joey ended, I got in touch with Karl. By that time, his wife had passed away. So again, I went back to D.C. to work at the Silver Slipper for Sam Shanker, and Karl came into town. We spent five beautiful days together. We decided that enough was enough: too many years had passed without us being together. At that point, there was no reason why we couldn't be together: we became engaged. I had of course told Sam about the engagement as well as a girl that was the Mistress of Ceremonies on the show, Rea Parker. Well, Rea was also a singer. Karl's and my song was "I Wish You Love," so every night she would sing "I Wish You Love." That night, we decided, "this is it." We called up Cyrese and told her, "We're *finally* engaged, after *all* these years, and we're *finally* going to be together." Cyrese had never met Karl, but she had talked to him on the phone before. By then, she was in her twenties and close to marriage herself. She knew how much I loved him.

I was going to make all the arrangements. We decided to get married on my birthday, June 18, in 1978. He said, "We'll get married in Las Vegas." A few months after that, he said that he wanted to get away completely from the Teamster business: he said that we were going to go away and that we should stay away for at least two years. We were planning on going to Australia. He had always wanted to go to Australia and see the Great Barrier Reef. So that was our plan. He wanted to get away from his work and I was going to get away from mine. I even did a "Farewell Tour" and retired from burlesque about six months before the wedding.

After my last performances, I went back to New Jersey where I had a home at which Cyrese was living. I was trying to decide what to do: I hated leaving Cyrese. Even though she was an adult, I still wanted to be there for her. She was also thinking of getting married and I wanted to be part of that celebration. Here was Cyrese in New Jersey, and I'm thinking: *Oh my goodness, you know, how am I going to do all this? I'm going to be away from my daughter.* At the same time, I knew I loved Karl. It was Big Decision Time, again. I also had decided to get away from show business for a while to do something else. I needed to decide if I really wanted to travel for two years in order to marry Karl. So once I got home, I took a job as a bartender in Bordentown, NJ.

While I was there, Jeff Edmiston came in. He was a nice young man who was twelve years younger than me. We would talk for hours. He ended up coming in every day, and I couldn't figure out how he was able to spend so much time with me. Jeff would sit and talk with me and sometimes take me out for breakfast after my shift. I told him that I was engaged to Karl, who was in California. Boldly, he asked me why I wanted to marry a Teamster. I said that it was because I was in love with a Teamster! I also had friends, Joan and Pete Biocco, who were trying to talk me out of marrying Karl. They asked me how I could just sell my home, move to California for a while, and then leave the country for two years. They just couldn't understand how I could go abroad for twenty-four months and have no contact with anyone. They thought I should marry a nice, down-to-earth guy like Jeffrey and settle down; they thought I should lead the normal life I never had and always wanted.

There was a big Teamsters meeting in Miami Beach in January 1978 and Karl sent me airline tickets to meet him there for three days. We had scheduled our wedding to take place on June 18th of that year. I told Jeff; I said, "I'm going to Florida because Karl sent my tickets." I told him bluntly that I was in love with Karl and wanted to be with him all the time. So I went to Florida and spent beautiful days with

Karl. We went to some of the Teamster functions, and on one evening Karl got up and announced our engagement to the whole convention. Everyone was so happy for us. I told Karl that I didn't want a big diamond engagement ring — all I wanted was a plain band of gold. He had brought to Florida a band of gold and a beautiful, beautiful solid gold, heart-shaped necklace on a thick rope chain. On the necklace, he had engraved my real name, Velma, and on the other side, it read, "I Wish You Love."

That was a beautiful time. We were so in love. One night, we were having dinner at a place called "The Caves" in Fort Lauderdale. Their card read, "We are at the Caves. Try to find us." It was a very romantic place, dark like a cave, with little private nooks for tables. After dinner, Karl rented a car and we drove out to the beach; there, we talked and stayed to watch the sun rise. I said, "You know, we should get married right here in Miami. I mean it. Right now."

He said, "But sweetheart, we've planned the wedding for Vegas and set the date and made all of the arrangements."

I said, "I don't know. I just got a feeling that it should be now." I didn't tell him about meeting Jeff or about what my friends wanted me to do. So anyway, he said it was a good thought but that we only had a few months more to wait; he said that we should stay with our plans and get married on my birthday. I said "okay" — reluctantly. When it was time to go, we were both at the airport. He went back to Los Angeles and I went back to New Jersey. I had such a strong feeling that I should just go with him. But I didn't. I cried most of the way back to Jersey.

When I got back, my friends continued to lobby for Jeff. And Jeff was pleading with me, saying. "You can't marry him. You have to marry me." Continuously, I said, "I love him. We've waited for years to be together." But Joan was relentless in her campaign for Jeff: she asked one day that I sit down and write a "Dear John" letter to Karl, stating that I couldn't marry him and that I didn't want to leave New Jersey and the country for two years. She said that I didn't have to send it and that it would just clarify how I really felt. I wrote the letter, put it in an envelope, and addressed it to Karl at his Teamster office in Los Angeles. But I had *no intention of sending that letter*: what I didn't know was that Joan came back and took the letter and mailed it. Here I am walking around with every intention in the world of marrying Karl, but then there was this letter in the mail that said I couldn't go through with the wedding. She told me about it after a week or so.

This was the hardest section to write about. How do you explain how you can love one man with every fiber of your being for years and then marry someone else that you hardly know, let alone love? But that is what I did. I could have just called Karl and explained the letter: it was a stupid prank to get a friend off my back. Instead, I let them talk me into marrying Jeff. I was two hours late for the ceremony on March 2, 1978. I told Cyrese that I didn't think I was doing the right thing: I loved Karl. Why did I *ever, ever* sit down and write that letter? I said, "I'm just doing the wrong thing." But after much agonizing, I went through with the ceremony. Jeff and I went to Mexico City and Acapulco for our honeymoon, but all I did was sit and think of Karl and what he must have thought when he got that letter. After the honeymoon, Jeff and I went back to Yardville, New Jersey, where I had been living. One day, I got a call from Karl: he was in San Juan, Puerto Rico, and he was really drunk. He finally had the courage to ask me how I could have sent that letter despite the way we had loved each other. I explained what had happened and told him that I just didn't have the courage to explain. He wanted me to just drop everything, to leave Jeff, and to fly to San Juan to meet him. I tell you, I wanted to go: I wanted to pack up and go to him. But I didn't. Sometimes, I still regret not marrying Karl. I still think about him every day.

I saw Karl one other time when I went to visit my cousin in California. I called him at his office in Los Angeles and told him that I was in the area. We had lunch and both had tears in our eyes when we met. He was married again and I was married to Jeff. He told me that he would always love me and that maybe someday we could work things out. He took me to the airport when I left and took a picture for both of us. When I got home, I was so happy that I saw him. I would always love him, but I chose another life and stuck with that decision. I am sure that old fears played a large part in this:

I would have been alone with Karl for two years; would he still have loved me as Velma Fern, or would he eventually become bored with the farm girl that he didn't know?

It is now thirty-eight years later and Jeff and I are still married. I finally made it work with someone. He and I are very different and we fight a lot, but we don't walk away. We are companions in our journeys. That is probably what has made the difference: he accepts who I am and never tries to change me.

These are my love stories. There are many, but remember that my career involved meeting men and flirting with them every day. Like Elizabeth Taylor, I married eight times. Neither Liz nor I should have married so easily and frequently. I shouldn't have married men that I didn't love in a romantic way. I did love Benny, Jack Johnson, Manny, and Karl. I was very fond of some of the others, too—especially Charles Butler. I am now at peace with my past and thankful for the memories. People ask if I ever had a big wedding and I didn't, but twice I did get married in a church (to Fred and to Jeff.) I now know that in the end God makes sure that we end up where we are supposed to be. And here I am.

I have accumulated a lot of pictures over the years, but for some reason I do not have many of my husbands and loves. This picture, at least, was taken by Charles in the late 1950s while we were on vacation in Miami.

This picture was taken in our house in Miramar. We were dressed and ready to go to the country club for dinner.

I went to England to get away from the "Manny Mess." I never felt at home and was miserable the whole time I was there. However, it was an amazing experience and I learned a lot. I just didn't get over Manny as planned. This was the outside of the apartment building where I lived.

In my very British flat, where you put a coin in a meter to get heat. I was not warm the whole time I was there.

This is the Arthur Fox Revue Bar in Manchester. It was one of the nicest nightclubs in England.

Went to see the Queen; they didn't let me in. Just kidding. Here I am at the changing of the guard at Buckingham Palace.

Cyrese and me with Jerry Vale at the Cedar Gardens Night Club in Trenton, NJ in 1977.

Karl and me at "The Cave" in Miami Beach, Florida in January 1978. This was the same night that I begged him to marry me. But he said we should wait to my birthday in June. The wedding day never came.

Jeffrey and me at our wedding in 1978.

Nicole, Jeffrey, and me at the Mirage in Las Vegas. We took her on a trip to show her the places that I worked. This night is a wonderful memory.

My Career In Photos

Sometimes it is so much better to tell a story with pictures. My time in burlesque is like that. Dancers were required to have portfolios of publicity photos. In addition, some clubs took their own photos to use in local advertising or to sell to customers. I have included some of my publicity photos and pictures of my performances. They show my life in burlesque better than my words ever could.

We all had head shots that were suitable to use in all settings.

This is from the Finale of the Minsky show at the Manor Hotel, Wildwood, NJ.
The Finale was the like a Grand March at a prom (never went to one of those) and
was frequently called a Parade of Stars. The dress was a shocking pink. I loved it.

This is the small bench that I frequently used as a prop in my act.
I would decorate it and use it with different themes and routines.

In 1961: I was performing at the Picadilly Club in Miami Beach and being just a bit naughty.

From the early 1960's: the picture shows me flirting with the audience. I would always look the men right in the eye and wink at their wives. The wink showed that I respected her territory and had no intention of going any further.

On stage in the
1960's.

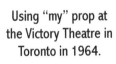

Using "my" prop at
the Victory Theatre in
Toronto in 1964.

A fur stole is so nice for a girl on a cool night. I always loved mine.

At some point, though, a girl is going to get hot. Right??

This was a publicity photo taken in the mid-1960s. Years later, it was this picture that appeared in Penthouse.

Publicity photo taken in the mid-1960s.

Posing with Ann Corio and the
Comedians from her show
This Was Burlesque in the mid-1960s
in New York City.

With Harold Minsky, Charlie Robinson, and
Murray Brisco in New York City, 1964.

Me and my prop in the mid-1960s
performing in Myrtle Beach, SC.

This is Rose La Rose and me at her home
in Toledo, OH, in 1964. I was working at
the Town Hall Theatre that she owned. In
many ways, Rose was my mentor. She was
also the most daring dancer that I knew:
she got away with more than I ever tried.

Christmas in Burlesque. A fun time and—of course—you needed a red cape with fur trim and the undergarments to go with it. I really did love my Christmas routines.

Getting ready to go on in Rose's Theatre in late 1960s. The stole was always with me.

A few publicity photos from the 1970s.
I was going more for the dark colors as I got older.

Chapter Six

So Many Wonderful Memories

In the late 1950s and 1960s, an evening at a burlesque club was a wonderful night out. You would come in and be seated by the Maître D' just like in a restaurant. Cocktails would be served and the comic or MC would go on first. They would do a comedy routine, usually with a female partner. The girl would be a comic foil to the MC. Back then, the comic got lots of laughs without being dirty or using bad language. It was all implied, you know, a double entendre; it was suggestive but not embarrassing. Then, the girls would perform individually with the lead performer to come on last. There could be two or three shows a night, music playing between sets for dancing. In the fancy clubs, there was a band; in the others, a sound system would play the music. The audience would consist of a mixture of couples, groups, and single (as in *alone*) men.

By the 1960s, I was always the headliner and would perform last. I loved burlesque. There were so many wonderful things about it back then. I want to describe the places I went and the people I met. But first, let's talk about how I became known as the First Lady of Burlesque. It was the early 1960s and Jackie Kennedy was the First Lady. Well, everyone said that I looked like her: I had big eyes and dark hair that I wore in a flip. In addition, the reviewers said that I had elegance and class like the first lady. So they started calling me the "First Lady of Burlesque." No one ever objected. After all, I was one of the few entertainers that never claimed to have slept with the President and I think everyone appreciated that.

Travel is part of the job in burlesque. In my early career, I stayed mostly in the central part of the country. This was especially true when Cyrese was small. As I said, I performed in Texas, Oklahoma, Kansas, and New Mexico. There were also several contracts that took me to Mexico. Basically, your agent would book you and off you went. Then, when I moved to Florida, I performed in the Miami area but had other bookings throughout the state. After that, there was Washington D.C., New York City, Boston, and clubs all over New Jersey. I also performed in California, Las Vegas, and various other cities on the West Coast. I have been to England and Canada. In other words, if you wanted to see the world you didn't have to join the Navy, you could become a burlesque dancer. There is a list of some of the clubs and theatres where I performed in the Appendix.

My favorite place to perform was a theatre, particularly in the Minsky and Ann Corio shows, as well as the B&E circuit. These were like the Ziegfeld Follies. I was on the stage like a real performer, which everyone said I was. This was entertainment: there were all sorts of acts and the camaraderie amongst the cast was strong. You were a member of the troupe, even if you were the star. Harold Minsky was known for doing nudity in a "nice way." Many famous comics started with these shows, including Phil Silvers and Robert Alda. Their stage is also where Gypsy Rose Lee and Ann Corio started.

Minsky liked to wine and dine and flirt with me. He was trying to convince me to star in his new show in Las Vegas. And, oh, I met *so* many people through these shows. Bobby Rydell used to come in every night. He was a very young man and a big star with a great voice. He had such a great big crush on me. He would come in every night and catch my show — from the wings and everything. We would go into the coffee shop and have a Coke or a cup of coffee or something like that. He was so, so cute. I still think he was singing Volare just to me. And I met Fisher and Marx, the comedy team. I became extremely close friends with Lou Marx. He was the comic and Al Fisher was the straight man. They worked Vegas a lot as Frank Sinatra's opening act. They worked with Sammy Davis,

Jr. and they hung around and worked with the whole Rat Pack. Oh, the stories I heard from Louie! I called him "Little Louie," and every time I would go into a club to see *them* perform, he'd stop what he was doing on stage, look at me, and he'd just say, "Tooooooooooo much!" and then go on with his act. We remained friends for *years*.

After I left the Minsky show and between my Yonkers and Wildwood bookings, I starred in the Ann Corio show, *This Was Burlesque*. There, I met Jim Henson and his wife. He contacted Dave Cohn, my agent in New York City at the time, and I wound up working for him with a part in the film *Timepiece*. I am the only person in burlesque that has ever been in a Jim Henson film—and that movie was a 1965 Sundance winner and an Academy Award-nominee. I played myself, a burlesque dancer, and wore one of my own costumes. It is still a cult movie to this day, depicting an ordinary man in constant motion who tries to escape the passage of time. It won an award at the Cannes Film Festival, and what he did with that film, which is such an *odd* film, is still being taught at every college in the world. It's a hard film to describe: it's about time, I guess, going so fast, and about people not knowing what they're doing. Really, if you can, you should see it.

When I started working the burlesque circuit, I made about $600 a week. As I gained popularity, I was making up to $1,000 a week. As a headliner, I made over $1,000, each salary negotiated by an agent. After the film and the

Minsky and Corio circuits, my salary escalated again. When talking about the good things about burlesque, you can't forget why we all did it: it was for the money and to make a living. For me, though, it was also about the applause. I was able to buy my first car (and, yes, I got my license first— really!) I bought a used Oldsmobile '98 just before a trip to Chicago. As I checked into the hotel, someone bumped into the car and pushed it right into a crosswalk. The car was impounded and towed before I came out to get my luggage. I bought my first new car, a Pontiac convertible, in Tulsa while I working at the Stardust club. I really loved that car. Owning a car gave me a degree of independence that I liked. I am also the only burlesque star to have had a feature article in Sports Illustrated. When I was in the Corio shows, Ann threw a welcoming party for me where I met one of the editors of Sports Illustrated. I told him that I wanted to be in his magazine: he said that he didn't think so, explaining that burlesque wasn't their kind of sport. I told him that I played golf and he responded that a lot of people play golf. We were both having fun with the back and forth, but then I told him that I had an eight handicap. He was dumbfounded and told me that he doubted it was true. I said that if he played with me I could beat him by several strokes. He didn't say anything, but he called a couple of weeks later and set a play date at the Westchester Country Club. However, he sent an associate editor who played very well to play with me. I beat him by three strokes and got my feature article in Sports

Illustrated. It was so important to keep your name in the public eye — and I worked hard to keep my name out there.

After I completed my contracts with Anne Corio and the Minsky shows, Jake Samara asked for my help back in Oklahoma City. He had run into some financial and tax problems and lost all his clubs. He was ready to open a new spot called the Stage Door but didn't have the money to pay a headliner. He asked me to come home and perform for him. Of course, I said yes. Burlesque people help each other in situations like this. When I was in town, two reporters from the Daily Oklahomian did a feature story on me. I had worked with both of them when I was a copy girl and we had a great time catching up.

Finally, I am the only burlesque star to ever perform at a major university. I performed at the Irvine Auditorium at the University of Pennsylvania. Before the show, I was interviewed by the Dean. I always dress elegantly for interviews: I never wear anything showing a décolletage (or anything like that) and I never wear much makeup. After talking to me, he was enthusiastic about the show. That, too, was good publicity; the students and faculty were a wonderful audience. I would go back there in a minute.

One of my most special moments was when I met Martin Luther King Jr. I so admired him and what he was trying to do. I always believed that all people were equal and tried to treat everyone the same, but I knew that everyone did not agree with me about this. I met Martin Luther King Jr.

and Ralph Abernathy when I was on a plane to Charlotte, North Carolina. A mutual friend introduced us and I had the chance to tell him how much I supported him. I even asked him for an autograph! That night, I was performing at this big club to a packed house and I was still on a high from that morning. I really intended to tell the audience about how thrilled I was to meet the civil rights leader, but the music started and I went into my act. *No problem*, I thought. *I will tell the story before the next show.* But between shows, one of the other dancers told me that the audience was filled with members of the Ku Klux Klan, including the Grand Wizard for the State. God was really watching over me that night! My little announcement would have started a riot.

Another time, I was on a plane returning home from Green Bay, Wisconsin. Jimmy Durante was sitting across the aisle from me. We had both brought cheese back with us; he had limburger and I had cheddar. We started joking about the smell permeating through the plane and then continued to talk about burlesque. We talked the entire way home. And, I never apologized to the four nuns sitting behind us who were listening intently the entire time. Our conversation wasn't exactly "g" rated.

Wherever you perform, the show business community sticks together, going to each other's shows and having parties together. You meet a lot of people, some famous and some everyday folk. We all basically lived together when we were in the same town. I don't want to just list the people I met, but I do want to talk about some funny stories involving stars you may know. I also want to talk about some of the non-stars that were so important to me.

One of the first stories involves a strange incident and Jerry Vale. I was at home in Trenton with my daughter, not working for a few weeks, when Joe Fachone (who owned a local supper/nightclub called Cedar Gardens) called me and said, "April, how would you like to bring your daughter and come over to see Jerry Vale perform?" He said, "I'll introduce you." So I said, "Oh, fine." I figured that he was supposed to be a pretty nice guy; he was married to a stripper by the name of Rita Grabel who I sort of knew, anyway. So Cyrese and I dressed up and went to Cedar Gardens.

We had a front row table. Jerry went on and sang; I had always been a great admirer of his voice. I thought he had a *fabulous* voice. After the show was over, Joe introduced us: he brought Jerry and his manager over to the table. He sat down and visited, and everything was nice. Jerry then went backstage to get ready for another show, when his manager came over and said, "Jerry wants you to meet him after the show, out at the Holiday Inn." And he says, "I'll give you the key to his room, and you can come over when he finishes his show. You should get there maybe an hour after the show is over." And I said, "Oh. Uh huh. Oh." So I took the key and already knew what I was going to do. I figured, you know, this is terrible. There are so many cheaters in the world, and here he's married to a *beautiful* girl. And I'm thinking, "What if that was me, what if I was married to him and he did that to me?" Besides, I had my daughter with me. So anyway, I fixed him. He thought I was going to show up. I threw the Holiday Inn key in the trash and went home and forgot about it. I was no longer a fan of Jerry Vale's. I liked his voice, but I didn't like him.

Meeting Desi Arnaz and Judy Garland was another catastrophe. I am sure that neither would have remembered meeting me ten minutes after I left. I was working the Piccadilly Club in Miami Beach, where I'd become friends with Zorita, the owner of Zorita's around the corner. It was really hard to make woman friends and I treasured the ones I had. One morning, she called and asked me to go to breakfast with her. She said she'd pick me up in her vintage Rolls Royce. And so she, her girlfriend, and a drunken Desi Arnaz picked me up and we drove over to a restaurant. There, a drunken Judy Garland waited for us with a doctor-friend of Zorita's, as well as a couple of other people that I didn't know. Pauly Dash, the comedian at my club was there, too. I sat and had breakfast. Everybody was pretty well sloshed (except Zorita, she didn't drink that much.) And Judy Garland, oh my goodness, she swore like a sailor. As for Desi Arnaz, he was like *slobbering* all over the place. So I thought, "Holy cow, these people are so famous and so *wiped out*." They asked if I wanted to go party after breakfast and I said no. I said, "I'm going home. I'm a little tired. But, it was nice meeting everyone." This incident is symbolic of how hard it was to be continuously on the road entertaining: many just drank and partied all the time and only lived a normal life when home.

Let's move on to a nicer story. One evening, I was getting ready to go on stage at the Piccadilly Club again, for Sam Shanker. Sam came back to the dressing room and asked if I'd like to come out to meet Martha Raye. He said that Martha Raye was in the audience with her attorney, and she would like to meet me. So I went out to the table and sat down with Martha: she was a very funny lady, and just a little inebriated. She ordered more drinks and asked me if I'd like one, to which I said okay. I ended up having several drinks and sat there for quite a while, talking, until I had to get ready to do another show. So I went back, got dressed, and it was show time and I was on stage. I was just getting on the bench, a prop that I used to lay down and take off some of my clothes: I took off my shoes, and then I laid them down on the bench to sit and remove my stockings. But when I had my legs up in the air, who walks onstage dressed like a maid with an apron and everything but Martha Raye. She came over and grabbed my panties and stockings off of the floor, and said, "Yes, Miss March. I'll wash these out and I'll have them for you first thing in the morning." And the people just *roared*. And I cracked up so bad that I started laughing. Here Martha Raye had come out and done that. It was a funny bit, and the place was packed and people roared, but I was laughing so hard that it was *very* hard to continue with the show. She was a real classy lady.

Another funny incident occurred when I was working at the Hillside Theatre in Jamaica, Queens. They were announcing me: the "First Lady of Burlesque," you know, the beautiful, exotic, First Lady. They gave me such a big buildup and everything. I go out, and I'm walking around, and I'm on the runway, and I'm acting every bit a grand lady and the First Lady of Burlesque. And so I go back to lay down on the prop, and lo and behold, Tommy Moe Raft (the head comic on the show) had opened up the curtain in the back of my prop and put a whoopee cushion on there. I knew *nothing* at all about it, either, and I sat down and this *loooooooud* fart sound comes out of the cushion. The audience roared and I, again, just cracked up. I laughed so hard but it was so *embarrassing*; Tommy stuck his head out from behind the curtain and came out with a "Ha Ha Ha Ha Ha!" in a high voice. You just never knew what would happen.

That reminds me of other funny things that happened. At the Roxy, the announcer would yell out, "And here is the glamorous First Lady of Burlesque, Miss April March." Once, I started walking down the runway and I tripped: I tripped on the linoleum part of the runway and fell into the band pit. I almost — almost, mind you — shattered the drums to pieces. That was quite an embarrassing moment for me, but I picked myself up, dusted myself off, and on I went. I got back up on that runway and finished the show. You know the show has to go on. I was a little bit bruised from the fall, but otherwise in good shape.

I fell off the stage only one other time. I was performing at the Follies Theatre in San Francisco. In between shows some of the comics convinced me to go across the street with them for a few drinks. I still didn't drink that much but went for the company. They were such a nice group. I ended up having five frozen margaritas. I was so drunk! I went back, walked down the runway and right off the end. Never drank between shows again. It became a rule.

Once when I was in Dayton, OH, I went out with a group from our theatre to catch the act of singer Tommy Leonetti. He was appearing in a nightclub. With Tommy was onstage, I walked in and sat down at a front-row table. People were gasping when I walked in: I had worn this beautiful, *beautiful* white, clingy dress with a chiffon top and a chiffon hood with rhinestones all around it. With my black hair and that white dress with the rhinestones, I looked quite striking. Plus, I was wearing my long, white fox stole. When I walked through the club, people were all watching and admiring *me* instead of listening to Tommy Leonettti. So after his show was over, he came over and introduced himself and said, "Miss March, you *certainly* know how to upstage an act!" And I laughed, and I said, "Well, I didn't mean to. I just came nicely dressed." After the show was over, we spent the night together and went to breakfast in the morning. He came to the theatre and watched my show the following day, and he invited me out to catch his act the following night. He was just a lovely man and a gentle lover.

So many people were important to me. I met Joe DiMaggio at the Jockey Club in Washington, D.C.: a friend, Pete Genarris, introduced us at a luncheon at the Jockey Club. We became wonderful friends. Joe and I had so much in common, including our favorite drink, a Bloody Mary and our favorite champagne, Dom Perignon. Once, we drove all over Washington looking for a bottle early in the morning. There were rumors that he was involved with many women, but he was mourning the death of Marilyn Monroe and had eyes for no one else. He was really a shy, quiet man who was hurting very badly. I did love him, but not in a sexual way. We were wonderful friends.

Pete introduced me to a lot of Washington movers. Once, he introduced me a man that worked in the Nixon administration and later for Ronald Reagan. This man was a political strategist whose picture had been on the cover of *Time*; he was very interested in me. I finally agreed to have dinner with him: we had a lovely meal at a Georgetown restaurant and went back to his apartment for a drink. When we arrived there, he excused himself to get something in the bedroom. I stood looking at the city view from his apartment and thought that I had really arrived. He then called me into the bedroom to "show me something." I thought it was cute that a man of his stature would use this old come-on line. I slowly opened his door to see a room full of S&M equipment. I grabbed my fox stole off his sofa and ran. The stole was the only piece of clothing that I took off that night and I snuggled in it in the cab all the way home.

Pete also asked me to help a friend of his pick out a birthday gift for his wife. His name was Louie Belson and he was married to Pearl Bailey. The three of us went shopping and picked out a beautiful pair of gold and pearl earrings. Afterwards, I frequently would see her wearing them in publicity photos and would always think that we had made a good choice.

When I would return to certain clubs for repeat performances, I would socialize with certain friends that I would see for dinner. Many had been or would become life-long friends. For example, I knew the judge in the second Sam Sheppard murder trial in Cleveland. I had dinner with him every time I was at The Roxy Theatre in Cleveland.

Years before in Wichita, Kansas, I was working at the T-Bone Supper Club when a gentleman walked in, saw the show, and arranged to meet me after the show's end. I went out to get a cup of coffee in the club and he came over to me and introduced himself: he was Russell Arms, the singer from the old Hit Parade show, with Giselle McKenzie and Snookie Lanson and that group. We became friends, and I had several dates with him while he was in Wichita. Another lovely person. It seems like I was kind of drawn to singers. In later years, there was Mel Torme and, well, Tommy Leonetti, and Russell Arms.

When I was at the Hillside Theatre in Jamaica, Queens, I missed a show because I had done the Joe Franklin Radio Show in New York City. I was on air with Cecily Tyson,

Joe Walt, the world's strongest man, and Joe Frazier, the heavyweight champion of the world. After the show was over, I had to get back to do a show at the Hillside Theatre — but I decided that I wanted to try the subway instead of taking a taxi. I ended up on the wrong subway train. Realizing I was lost, everyone on the train became involved and told me to get off at different places. I wound up missing my first show. Needless to say, the theatre owner was quite unhappy: everybody got their money back since there was no April March there to do the show. I got lectured about that, and I never took a subway train in New York afterwards because I was afraid that I would miss another show. But the following day, Joe Frazier came out to the theatre to catch the show. I had some lovely times visiting with him.

Another time, I was supposed to do the "To Tell the Truth" show in NYC. I had been working at the Mayfair Theatre for Leroy Griffith. I had a meeting with Goodson Toddman, during which they said that they wanted to set up a date for me to tape that week. Because I had to ask Leroy, I said that I would have to let them know: I needed to know if I could take off to go and tape the show. But Leroy said, "You can't. You're the star of my show. You have to be here for every performance." I said, "You'd get a million dollars' worth of publicity out of this, because I would say where I'm working this week." Still, he said no. "You can't do the show while you're working for me." So I had to cancel even though I really wanted to do the show. I was angry about this for a long time.

When I worked at clubs in Washington, Wilbur Mills would often be in the audience. I got to know him fairly well and he did pursue me for a while. Thank goodness I never got involved with him. To get him off my back, I introduced him to Fanny Fox—and we all know what happened there. Oh well, I was just trying to be nice. But one of my favorite memories unfolded at the Silver Slipper club in Washington, D.C. where Rea Parker, the singer/MC, was my wardrobe catcher. I paid a small fee each week for her to pick up my wardrobe as I took it off and hang it up in my dressing room. She was a heavyset woman who became my good friend over the course of the many times that I came to star at one of the clubs owned by Sam Shanker: the Celebrity Room, The Paper Doll, The Silver Slipper, and the Plaza Theatre. We remained friends until she died of heart failure in the 1970s. Ree had a young son, Junior, who would later die from AIDS at a young age in Philadelphia. Ree would always sing Karl's and my favorite song, "I Wish You Love," each time he came to town for a Teamster's meeting.

In Washington, D.C., I met the most interesting man. Ronald Reagan was President and there was such excitement in town. I was working at the Silver Slipper when one of the waitresses came in and said that a man gave her a $100 tip to ask me to come out and have a drink with him. I went to the table and saw this funny looking man: he was short and Polynesian-looking, wearing so many mismatched plaids that you just had to stop and look. He had a plaid tam on his head with a red tassel on top. In a weird way, he was cute and adorable. I sat down and we ordered drinks; we talked for a long time. He said that he was the King of the Marianna Islands and that he was in town to meet with President Reagan. After our chat, he asked if I would meet him the next night for an early dinner. I agreed because I really liked him.

The next night, he sent a car to bring me to the Washington Hilton. We ate at Trader Vic's and again had a lovely time. We got a lot of stares during the meal which didn't bother me at all. He said that he was leaving the next day to return home, and asked for my home address so that he could send me a small gift. About six weeks later, I received a box at my home in New Jersey containing a beautiful handbag made out of palm tree leaves. He had also included a long letter in which he asked me to join him on an all-expense paid vacation to his islands. I told him that regretfully, I couldn't go. He then sent a series of letters describing how people lived in his country. On the Islands, there was no TV or any other entertainment source; the women all wore grass skirts and the men wore sarongs. He told me that he would like to teach me to spearfish and felt that we could be very happy together. I couldn't see myself living like that and continued to say no. Still, it was fun to think of myself roaming around his islands, dressed in a grass skirt and my fox stole and nothing else.

Then, there was the roast in Wayne, New Jersey in 1982. That was a big deal, because there weren't too many women who were ever roasted by the Circus Saints and Sinners: they had only roasted Edie Gorme, Gypsy Rose Lee, Elizabeth Taylor, Ann Corio, and ME! All the other people, generally the Circus Saints and Sinners, usually just roast sports figures — the big name sports figures. So I felt very privileged and honored to have been chosen to be roasted. It was one of the most special nights in my life. I still treasure the plaque and have lifetime privileges at the club. All of the money raised that night went to the Cancer Society.

Some of the other comics and straight men that I worked with included: Jimmy Matthews; Jimmy Pinto; Charlie Robinson; Tommy Moe Raft; Artie Lloyd; Art Unger and his wife, Barbara Curtis; Willie Dew and Ilke deCava; Billy Cheese-and-Crackers Hagen; Maxie Furman; Dick Richards; Lou Askell and his wife (who was also a stripper); Petty Dane; Billy Reed; Billy Ainsley; Dexter Maitland; Ben Hamilton; Lee Gifford; Harry Ryan; Lee Stewart; Al Baker, Sr.; Fisher and Marx; Professor Irwin Corey; and Ish Kabibble from the Kay Kaiser band. They were all wonderful individuals.

Another time, I was working at the Talk of the Town night club in Tucson, Arizona. Ish Kabibble was there too working as the Master of Ceremonies and he introduced me to Hoot Gibson who starred in cowboy movies and Wally Maddox, a movie producer. They saw my show and immediately after offered me a part in a movie that they were doing for Republic Pictures. They also offered me a long-term contract with that company. I thought that they were phonies and joking with me so I ignored them. I never told anyone that I didn't know who they were and Ish Kabibble thought I just turned down the offer. I would have refused even if I knew it was true . By this time, I was established and happy in Burlesque.

I also worked the Troc Theatre in Philadelphia with house comic Maxie Furman, who would later go on to Ann Corio's show, *This Was Burlesque*. Steve Mills and Jimmy Matthews, Harry Connolly and Dexter Maitland also worked with me in the Corio show. Jimmy was a *very* close friend until he died, years later, in Las Vegas. In fact, I spoke with him two days before he passed away. We were very special close friends. I still really miss him.

Then, of course, I met Kaitlyn Regehr, the producer of Slice TV in Toronto. She had Meredith Smart, a food blogger friend of hers, develop the "April March Cocktail". It is on the menu in several bars in Toronto, including the famous Cadillac Lounge. The recipe for the cocktail is in the Appendix. It is pretty and tasty — and it has quite a kick, just like me. Nurse it, because one is more than enough. I freely share the recipe with hotels and restaurants that I visit and with friends and family. I hope you enjoy it.

There was an attorney in Washington, D.C. who let me use a free apartment in his hotel whenever I was in town. The apartment remained unoccupied whenever I wasn't there. He gave me the apartment for free just to get me to go and have lunch with him every day. He took me to wonderful restaurants and took me shopping for furs. He loved being seen around town with me. He would also take me sightseeing to all of the famous places in Washington, D.C.

In Springfield, Missouri, I would spend time with a doctor in his eighties who was the Head of the Chiropractic Association. No matter where I was, he would come to my opening nights. He always sent me a $100 bill for each year of my age on my birthday. From time to time, he would fly me into town for a few days: he loved taking me shopping, and showing me off to his friends.

I did a few shows at the Derby Club with Christine Jorgenson, the first woman to undergo gender change surgery. She was really quiet and kept to herself a lot, but she was a lovely person. I really felt sorry for her: she didn't seem at all at ease with what she had done even as she publicized it. Since I worked in Dallas a lot, Jack Ruby frequently tried to get me perform in his club. I always refused, and this goes to show that I could have good judgment at times.

Finally, people often ask me about the music I performed to. Honestly, over the years I have danced to almost anything you can name. When I first started, I used songs such as "Night Train" and "Temptation." Of course, songs with the word "April" were favorites, including "April Love," "April Showers," and "April in Paris;" I also had a song written for me called "Blues for April." I have always liked pretty songs and used many in my act, such as "Shangri-La," "Girl from Ipinema," and "Spellbound." My number for the stockings-and-garter-belt routine was "Barefoot Contessa," and I tap-danced to "Tea for Two" and "Lullaby of Broadway." I never did perform to "I Wish You Love," though: it was too special to Karl and me. It still has a special spot in my heart.

April March is a former burlesque dancer who appeared as the stripper in Jim Henson's 1965 short film *Time Piece*. March performed in burlesque from 1952 to 1978, headlining at Minsky's and elsewhere. A golfer, March was interviewed in *Sports Illustrated*.

The "First Lady of Burlesque" has been wowing audiences since she appeared in an Our Gang short at the age of 10. In 1952, working as a cigarette and flower girl at The Derby Club in Oklahoma, she impressed Barney Weinstein, the owner of a popular burlesque club. He hired her as a dancer and re-christened her "April March". In the 1950s April was wooed by Hollywood, but turned down offers from both the Columbia and Republic studios to stay in Burlesque. In her 30+ year career as a burlesque dancer, she traveled all over the world and performed before a wide variety of audiences. In 1963 she worked for Harold Minsky (one of the famous Minsky Brothers) and later appeared in Ann Corio's This Was Burlesque. A chance remark about her golf handicap at the press reception for that show caught the attention of a reporter. Her skill as a golfer and her time as the Vice-President of the Woman's Golf Association in Tulsa, OK landed her a feature in Sports Illustrated, making her the only exotic dancer to appear in that magazine. April retired from burlesque in 1978 and now lives in the capital district of New York state.

This was one of the publicity photos from the movie, *Time Piece*.

At the Saint and Sinnners' Roast in October 1982.

The trophy presented to me at the Roast. There were 500 people attending.

Cyrese and me at the Roast. Jeffrey took the picture.

12 • THE TRENTONIAN, THURSDAY MORNING, OCTOBER 28, 1982

And Roasted, Too

Ex-Stripper Gets Dressing Down

By MATT REILLY
Staff Writer

WAYNE, N.J. — "She's a lady — a real lady."

It was heard over and over again in describing April March (yes, that's the name!), the former burlesque queen turned Yardville housewife who was "roasted" this week by the Circus Saints and Sinners in Wayne.

Saints and Sinners is a fraternal organization originally conceived to help down-and-out circus performers and which now holds celebrity roasts to raise money for charity.

Chosen as the latest "Fall Gal" for a show to benefit the American Cancer Society, the statuesque Miss March, who billed herself as "The First Lady of Burlesque" in her performing days, was led by five gaily dressed clowns through a stag audience of several hundred well-wishers gathered at the posh Wayne Manor and received a standing ovation.

She was then treated to a five-course dinner, a burlesque show, complete with a baggy-pants comic, strip-tease, bump-and-grind music and blackout comedy sketches, and finally roasted by Saints and Sinners "Louse Biographer" Fred Boyd.

Born Velma Ferne Worden in Oklahoma City, she went to Dallas at 17 and lied about her age to get started in show business at the Theater Lounge, where owner Barney Weinstein gave her the name April March.

She worked the night club circuit in the West and Midwest as a headliner for several years before traveling to Miami.

"My act was sexy," said Miss March, "but dignified. Not like today. My philosophy was to leave a little something to the imagination."

It was in Florida that she was the personal guest of King Saud of Saudi Arabia, who had come to this country for eye surgery. Saud was so taken by her beauty and charm that he wanted to whisk her away with him, but she politely declined.

In 1963 Miss March took her act to Manchester, England, returning after a few years to hit the burlesque theater circuit.

Her big break came when her agent in New York City got her an audition with the famous Harold Minsky Show. She starred in two of Minsky's shows and between shows starred for six weeks in Ann Corio's popular off-Broadway show, "This Was Burlesque."

It was during a press party thrown by Ms. Corio that a sportwriter found out that Miss March played golf to a 7 handicap (she had been vice president of the Womens' Golf Association at the Tulsa Country Club) and she became the first female exotic dancer to be written up in Sports Illustrated magazine.

Miss March worked nightclubs in Washington, where she had the dubious honor of introducing Congressman Wilbur Mills to one of her co-stars, stripper Fanne Foxxe, and the two became "headliners" of a different sort.

"Wilbur wanted to date me," said Miss March, "and I wouldn't go out with him, so I told him I'd introduce him to a nice girl."

During her career, she was wined and dined by the likes of baseball star Joe DiMaggio and actor Dale Robertson. She had been married four times before she met and married Jeff Edmiston, a ruggedly handsome independent trucker with whom she has made her home for the past five years.

Jeff had never seen a strip show until Miss March took him to one on their honeymoon, and roastmaster Boyd kidded that her husband was the only man who hadn't seen her with her clothes off.

Miss March has one daughter by a previous marriage, Cyrese, who owns and operates "Cyrese Bene," a hairstyling salon on South Broad Street, and a two-year-old granddaughter, Nicole Cyrese.

Asked if she would do it all over again, she said, "Not today. Today it's not show business, it's trash. If I could go back and do it in the days when it was fun I would. I was always elegantly dressed and did more teasing. Today they have everything off before they even come out."

Once asked by an interviewer what was the first thing the "First Lady of Burlesque" took off on stage, Miss March replied, "A lady always removes her gloves first."

April March...burlesque queen turned housewife

The article from The Trentonian describing the Roast. I was proud of the fact that I was one of a few women ever honored and that we raised a lot of money for the American Cancer Society.

A few more pictures from the Roast. It was really the best time. I always believed that you had to be able to laugh at yourself.

Chapter Seven

The Other Side of Burlesque

Just like everything else, burlesque has another side—a side that is not wonderful and that people do not talk about. The same things that made it amazing also made it awful. The people you meet are not always celebrities: they may be the individuals that you want to avoid at all costs. The places you go may be spots at which you have no desire being, and the constant travel can keep you away from the people you love. Being on the road all the time is not glamorous: rather, it is a challenge to the best of relationships. Yet to succeed, you have to do these things and keep smiling while you do them. You go on no matter what: that is show business.

To me, the worst thing about burlesque is what they call "mixing." Frequently, your contract would specify that between shows you had to "mix" with the audience. This meant that you had to work the room and sit and visit with the customers, encouraging them to buy you and others drinks. In other words, you were making more money for the owners. I hated this and, once I was successful, would insist that the clause be taken from my contracts. Better yet, when you performed in theatres, the need for this was eliminated. I preferred to spend the time between shows in my dressing room. It was safer. Still, sometimes you had to agree to mix in the clubs. But mixing was responsible for the worse night of my life: September 10, 1962.

The Place Pigalle

I was performing at the Picadilly Club in South Beach when Harry Ridge, the owner of the Place Pigalle down the street, offered me a better contract. In burlesque, performers frequently go from club to club for more money, a better environment, etc. The Place Pigalle was small and cozy. On a busy night, the audience consisted of about thirty to forty people. Harry had lost his headliner and was putting a new show together. The club had a live band that played for the performers and dancing, as well as Tony D'Arcy, a handsome young man with a beautiful baritone voice, Sharon Sutton, a young dancer and contortionist, and other burlesque dancers. Harry hired me as the lead stripper and a

Korean Singer, Lee Sohn, to bring in more customers. It was a small group and we all became extremely close in a short period of time.

I began at the Place Pigalle shortly after I divorced Charles Butler and just after I discovered that Manny Rabin was married. Cyrese and I were living in Mirimar, almost an hour north of Miami. I loved Miami and its diversity and the exposure to so many cultures. I rented a small room there for the duration of the contract, given that the Club closed late and it was a long drive home. So, I was with the other performers more than usual.

On the night of September 10, 1962, I had just finished my first show and was circulating through the audience. Two customers, one Korean and one American, were sitting with several of my coworkers. They asked me to join them and have a drink: it was my job to do this. I ordered a glass of my "favorite" champagne, which wasn't really my favorite as I didn't like to drink: as part of the mixing clause, though, they told me what to order. We sat and talked for a while, until the men were ready to leave. They asked for their bill and saw that it was over $300. That was when all hell broke loose.

The Korean customer, Kun-Wha Yoo, blew up. He said he only wanted to pay for the three drinks he ordered. He hadn't understood he was supposed to pay for the performers' drinks. The waiter insisted that he pay his bill. At that point, the customer lost his temper and the commotion caused the club steward to rush over to the table. Yoo and his friend finally ran out of the club and returned to their hotel, where Yoo loaded two guns, a .38 caliber snub-nosed revolver and a 4-inch barrel revolver. His friend tried to talk him out of going back to the club, but Yoo just left and took a cab back to the Place Pigalle. He arrived shortly before 2 AM.

Tony D'Arcy was standing outside to get some air and immediately recognized Yoo. He told him that he shouldn't go back into the Club; Yoo shot Tony twice in the belly. Then, doorman Dave Goodman tried to stop Yoo: Dave was seventy-three, but he stood in front of Yoo and told him that he couldn't go in. Yoo shot him twice in the legs. Pushing him aside, Yoo went into the club; Dave literally crawled behind him, bleeding all over as he continued to try to stop him. One of the dancers was onstage, but the music stopped. For a minute, there was such silence—and then everyone started screaming. The club manager yelled that Yoo was shooting blanks, and that there was nothing to be afraid of. This was a lie. The room was in a state of chaos. I was sitting in the back with Lee Sohn, our headline singer. I froze and stopped breathing; everything was a haze. When Yoo aimed his gun at Lee and me, Sharon Sutton, one of the dancers and my friend, threw herself in front of us and tried to hit him on the head. She was shot point-blank twice in the arm and once in the leg. Club Steward Hoffner grabbed a huge bongo drum and threw it at Yoo. It knocked him off-balance and the two began fighting.

When Yoo got free, he ran to the kitchen and stopped to reload his guns. It was there that Dave, the injured doorman, grabbed a prop machete and managed to hit Yoo in the head. It took two swings before Yoo went down, but the chaos was over. Tony was dead and Sharon and Dave were seriously injured.

Later, Yoo said that he really didn't want to hurt anyone: he just wanted to stand up for his rights and honor. He also said that he had been mad because he had been ill-treated by everyone at the club. He thought that this justified what he had done.

Police said that the club was a bloody mess, worse than anything they had ever seen. Although the doorman eventually recovered and returned to work at the club (bless him), Sharon did not fare as well. Several weeks after the incident, Sharon lost her leg. I felt terribly guilty: I picked her up from the hospital and tried to help her in any way I could. I did this for a long time. She told the newspapers that she was determined to dance again, but she never did. She just couldn't get over the trauma. About a year later, Sharon committed suicide.

Afterwards, I was a mess: I had difficulty coping with what we had all seen. One of the staff brought me to my agent's house where I stayed on his sofa for two days. I literally did not move. It was there that Manny found me. I was so glad that he was there, but at the same time I felt so guilty about our relationship. The next week leading up to Tony's funeral was a blur. But once I pulled myself together, I was determined to get out of Miami and Florida. It was then that I decided to go on a short cruise with a customer that I talked to at the Club, the lawyer of Fulgencia Batista. I was a wreck. When I got back to Miami, I learned that the police had discovered that both the shooter and his friend were wanted in Georgia for violent crimes and that they shouldn't have been running loose. The shooter was arrested for first-degree murder and his friend as an accessory to the crime. The incident was all over the press. One article in *True Detective* even called me a "femme fatale" and blamed me for the crime. I was so upset that I wanted to sue them, but my agent said that it would just cause more bad publicity.

The police used the shooting as a reason for declaring war on burlesque clubs in Miami and temporarily closed the Place Pigalle. When it reopened, burlesque was not allowed: we had to switch to belly dancing for a while. This was when I was arrested and later released. Miami also made it illegal for a club customer to buy a drink for the dancers, and the IRS began an energized and eager effort to audit the earnings of dancers. With all these changes, I felt that my life was falling apart: I quickly sold my house, went to Boston, and shortly after that traveled to England. Before that, though, we all had to testify in court for Yoo's murder trial. I will always remember his cold stare. He was found guilty of murder and attempted murder, and continues to serve a life sentence today.

You never really get over something like this. It stays with you and becomes part of your DNA. Nightmares, fears, and bad dreams become common: I ran from them, but they came with me. They *still* are with me. If I hear a car backfire, I panic. If I am in a public place and the power goes off, I have to leave. I don't like guns and fear being near anyone with a gun. I will never forget that night.

The Chicago Story

My second bad experience actually happened before the first but the shooting was definitely the more traumatic. When I got my first booking in Chicago, I was so excited that I bought my first car. The car was an Oldsmobile that I couldn't afford. Back in Oklahoma, I did some publicity photos for the dealership and got a reduced price. Driving up to the hotel, I parked the car and went in to register — but when I came out, the car was gone. It cost me plenty to get the car back from the police, and when I did, I should have just left. Really, I should have gotten in and sped out of that city. But sometimes I didn't do the smart thing.

In addition to my booking at the 606 Club, I pursued two specific things in Chicago: first, I wanted to work with Tony Midnight to design my first custom-made costumes; and second, I wanted to have a professional portfolio done by Maurice Seymour.

Tony Midnight was a talented, nationally-known female impersonator. He also happened to be a brilliant costume designer. Tony asked me to walk across the room to see how

I moved and then asked me to dance for him. It was almost like an audition. He wanted to create something that would flow when I moved and complement me and my routine. He thought of teal or turquoise to contrast with my dark hair and olive skin. I loved these colors.

He quickly came up with a design that I loved. The gown had tulle panels in a pale blue that revealed the turquoise dress underneath. It was low-cut in front, with jewels at the waist and shoulders to hide the tear-away points. Excited, I quickly set up a photo shoot with Maurice Seymour. Maurice had been working in Chicago since the 1930s. His photographs were just what I wanted: mysterious and sexy. This was my first professional photo shoot. Maurice really helped me so much: he taught me how to stand and move so that the pictures would be flattering. I ended up with a great portfolio and an education in how to look good for the camera. This was such a valuable lesson for a burlesque dancer.

After working with Tony and Maurice, I reported to work at the 606 Club. Like most of the clubs in Chicago and other big cities, the club was owned by the mafia. I knew it was best to keep my mouth shut and my eyes closed to anything unusual. If they liked you, it could mean more bookings; if they didn't like you, they would blackball you or worse. I was booked for seven nights a week for six weeks. Mixing was required, but I was not allowed to date or accept gifts from customers. There was one big exception, though: you were allowed to date and socialize with the mob bosses. If one of them wanted you to go out, you went out. No excuses allowed. I vowed to stay as far away from them as possible.

After my opening night show, I received a message that the Club's owner wanted me to join him at his table for a drink. He was a powerful boss who ran the city and much of the middle of the country. When I sat down, he looked me up and down like I was a prized racehorse. He was a bulky, intimidating man with a face like a bulldog. His eyes scared me: they looked menacing and I wanted to run. I decided that I'd see my contract through and then get out of town. He told me that I did good on the stage and ordered us drinks. Then, he asked me out for dinner on Sunday night. I lied and told him that I would love to but that I had to work on Sunday night: then, I excused myself for the next show. The next day, the club manager told me that I would have every Sunday night off. I went out with the owner that Sunday night and every Sunday for the following few weeks.

Tony was the mafia boss for everything west of the Mississippi. I didn't like him much but couldn't really say no to him either. During our dinners, I was just his arm candy. I sat and ate and he conducted business. I sat quietly and said and heard nothing while drug dealers, pimps, and other criminals paid Tony his share of their income. He told me to sit there, look pretty, and not to pay attention to what he did. Basically, these were "hear no evil, see no evil" nights. My engagement at the 606 was supposed to last six weeks; I just kept saying my prayers that I would make it through.

One night, "the boss" took me for a ride: after he finished his business, he showed me two diamond rings. He told me to pick one out—the one I didn't want would be the one he would give to his wife. *Great*, I thought. I smiled sweetly and picked one; I told him that his wife would love the other one. He didn't answer. That night, after dinner, I told him that I wanted to get some fresh air and walk back to my hotel. He wanted to come with me, but I told him I wanted some alone time. As I walked, I was suddenly aware that there were two men walking behind me. They seemed to follow me to the hotel. Petrified, I walked faster, realizing what a mistake it was to walk alone at night in Chicago.

When I got back, I ran in and went up to my room as quickly as possible. Looking out the window, I saw that the two were standing across the street, watching the hotel. They stayed there for a while and then signaled: a big black car picked them up. After that, I started to watch my surroundings more carefully and came to realize that two men usually followed me wherever I went. I began to receive strange phone calls in my room in the middle of the night, too. There was no doubt in my mind that Tony was having me followed. I was scared and anxious to move on. I should have just left.

On the following Sunday night, I asked Tony about it directly and he told me that they were his men. He said it was for my protection. I asked him to stop, but he said no.

The fear ratio increased tenfold: I *knew* that I was in a bad situation and that I needed to get out of town soon or else there would be no escape. I so wanted the contract to be over then and there. A few nights later, I received a note from the club manager to talk to him as soon as I could. I had been there five weeks, with one more to go. I was sure he wanted to talk about how to close out my contract. But when I went to his office, instead he calmly told me my contract had been extended indefinitely.

My heart literally stopped and it took me a few minutes to be able to respond. I told him that it wasn't possible: I had solid bookings elsewhere for the next several months. He responded that the extension came by way of Tony's request and that the other commitments had been taken care of. No other discussion allowed. A few hours later, my agent called and asked, "What the hell is going on up there?" He said that one of Tony's men had visited his office and threw a wad of bills at my agent. He told him that all of my future contracts "were canceled" and that I would be remaining in Chicago indefinitely. I started crying and asked the agent for help. He told me that I was the one that got involved with one of the biggest mob bosses in the country and that he wouldn't get involved for all the money I had. I was alone and going crazy. I could think of only one other person that could help.

A cop named Mike used to hang around the club: we had talked several times in the past, and he seemed like a stand-up guy. I thought that I could ask him what to do without worrying that he would tell Tony. So one night, I told him about my problems and asked what he thought I should do. Specifically, I asked him if I could just tell Tony that I was leaving. "April," Mike said, "you don't know what you are dealing with here." He said that no one leaves without consequences; he said that Tony's men had been known to throw acid in the faces of women who had tried to leave. He told me he was serious, dead-serious. I asked him for help but he said that he was afraid that we would get caught. We could both be killed or worse.

For the next few days, I was barely able to function. I needed to get out somehow, someway. Thankfully, Mike called one night after I got back to the hotel and said that he would help me. He "had a plan:" he told me I needed to follow it to the letter or else neither of us would make it. Over the next few days, I started taking a few things out of my dressing room each day. I would hide them in my purse, on my body, or under my coat so that nobody would see me walking out with my belongings. I went to a desk clerk at the hotel and told him that I would be checking out early the next morning and that I'd leave my luggage in the kitchen before I went to work. I paid him a lot of money to keep quiet. So I went to work, performed the worst I had ever performed in my life, and went back to the hotel. I was shaking with fear. After my escort left and the random call came, I went to the kitchen and out the back door. It was four o'clock in the morning. Mike met me with my car. He drove me to the edge of town and told me to keep going and not to look back. I was out of there and didn't look back or stop until I was in Missouri. In Missouri, I got out of the car and started shaking and sobbing. A trooper stopped and asked if he could help. After I told him my story, he said that I needed to get back in the car and keep driving. Mike didn't think that they would look for me until the next afternoon. In the meantime, I needed to get as far away from Chicago as fast as I could. I was going home and would never go back to Chicago again.

Once back in Oklahoma City, I stayed inside with my family for a long time and then started to go out a little bit. Jake Samara at the Derby Club talked me into joining his show for a few weeks. It was very low key, with no publicity; I was just there at night to perform. As I felt safer and more secure, I went on the road again, but I always looked over my shoulder. At first, I stayed fairly close to Oklahoma City and the tornado corridor. Then, I was brave enough to go back to the East Coast. After all, the East Coast Mafia and the Chicago group didn't get along and completely stayed out of each other's territories. I felt that I should be safe there.

After Chicago, I tried to stay away from mafia-owned clubs. But you really couldn't. So many clubs were owned by the mob. The men in Yonkers that wanted to "take care" of Joe really were darlings. But then there would also be groups like the one in Providence that wouldn't pay me because I refused to do "private shows" for the bosses. This time I went to the union and the bosses later came up with the cash. But otherwise, no one else held me prisoner or insisted that I stay with them. I thank God for this. By the time I retired, most clubs were owned by the Mafia and most dancers were just strippers who did bumps and grinds and took off all of their clothes.

Burlesque and the Law

Law enforcement had a love-hate relationship with burlesque. Officers frequented the clubs and, as in Chicago, many looked out for the dancers. But governments wanted to control the clubs and theatres and didn't want to leave it to the Mafia. After the shooting in Miami, I spent a night in jail wearing a belly dancers' costume and a raincoat. The police wanted to close all the clubs down. The charges were dismissed, but it wasn't a pleasant experience. Burlesque continued there and elsewhere.

I had one other run-in with the law in New York City in the early 1960s. I was performing at the 42nd Theatre. Between shows, I would return to my dressing room and read or rest. So, there I was in a leopard-print robe and slippers reading the paper when I heard loud shouts and the words, "This is a raid. Everyone is under arrest." I quickly turned off the lights and quietly locked my door. Moments later, the officers knocked it down. Everyone was arrested: stage hands, comics, and dancers. I had a ride in a paddy wagon (not as much fun as you would think) and wound up in what they called the "New York City Tombs." The tombs were known for their inhumane treatment of prisoners and it was there that we all spent the night. The next morning, the theatre owner posted our bail and told us to go back to the theatre right away so that it could open that night. In my robe, I took a taxi to a hotel, checked in, and took a bath. I took my sweet time going back to the theatre. Frequently, dancers were arrested like this for "lewd and lascivious behavior." The theatre owner would just bail us out and tell us to go back to work. This was not a positive aspect of the job, but it was part of it.

Loss of Family and Self

You had to make choices to be a burlesque star. You were on the road more than you were home and you worked really awful hours. Your family had to either put up with it or leave, or you had to leave in order to protect them. There is no way to have a normal family life and do what I did for a living. The most "normal" period in my life was when I was married to Charles Butler and lived in Tulsa. He was a wonderful man and we had an amazing life, but I needed my career and he didn't want other men gawking at me. He was the normal one and I couldn't be the wife he wanted. By then, burlesque was in my blood and couldn't be removed. I needed to be onstage.

No matter how many times I have said that I made all of my decisions with Cyrese in mind, she always felt that burlesque came first. I tried to keep her completely away from my work. Once when we were in New Jersey and I was still married to Joe, I received a call from the principal of her school. This lady was a stern-voiced nun who requested to see me as soon as possible. She made me wait for a long time in the outer office; I felt like a kid who was being called on the carpet. Once admitted, the nun wasted no time taking out one of the publicity photos in which I was scantily clad. Okay: I was wearing high heels, a fur stole, a g-string and nothing else. It was a good photo, though, and everything was properly covered.

Sister Mary Theresa told me that Cyrese had brought the photo to school and was showing the other students. I started blushing and stammering, truly embarrassed. I assured the nun who was sitting in judgment that my PR photos were locked in my desk at home and that I had no idea how Cyrese obtained a copy. She said that she questioned my upbringing of a child in a home where such photos were displayed. Then, she told me that all of the school staff would be watching for signs of neglect in Cyrese. Okay, now I was mad. I told the dear sister in no uncertain terms that I kept Cyrese completely away from my career and that *she* knew more about burlesque than Cyrese. When I was leaving, I couldn't help but ask if Sister Mary Theresa wanted me to sign the picture for her. If looks could kill, I would have been dead.

But to return to the topic at hand, Cyrese grew up with my grandparents, nannies, and neighbors. For every event of hers I made, there were four that I didn't. She blamed me for the abuse that she suffered at the hands of Joe Marion: she introduced us and adored Joe at first, but she didn't sign on for what happened. Even though I didn't know about it until much later, she blamed me and still has issues around this and my career. Although sometimes I think we are beyond it and "okay," there are other times when she will explode and all of those feelings will come streaming or screaming out. One of these recent outbursts was so bad that we are no longer on speaking terms. So at eighty, I am still fighting the ghosts of the past with my daughter. If I could make it okay, I would. But I really don't know how. We both need to accept the other as we are now, and move beyond the past. It just doesn't seem likely.

I was on the road when my mother and grandparents died and didn't find out about their deaths until months later. Nobody called me. I wasn't there for them and no one was there for me on those occasions and those nights that I wanted to be with my family so bad that it hurt. On the nights I wanted to be with and be there for Cyrese, I just cried. This, too, was part of the burlesque life: just the other side.

This is a picture of me belly dancing at the Place Pigalle after the shooting. It is the outfit that I was arrested in for indecent exposure.

In 1964, this was the costume and picture that I obtained from taking the booking at the 606 Club. This is the full costume.

The net skirt is removed in this one revealing the beautiful sheath underneath.

Down to my undies here. The flowers are a nice Spring touch.

Everything off, except the pasties and g-string. The fur shawl was always so helpful.

I did like to drop the g-string just before leaving the stage. Behind the curtain, I would wave a prop g-string and the audience would go wild.

A publicity photo from the famous 606 Club in Chicago:
wish Elliot Ness had been there to save me

Working the 606 Club on Wabash Avenue in Chicago at age 21.
Wearing a Tony Midnight Costume.

More publicity shots from the 606 Club taken in 1956.
I was 21 years old, too young to be dealing with the Mafia alone.

Chapter Eight

What Happened To Us All

Today, I am still married to Jeffrey and living in Upstate New York. I am known as Velma Edmiston and—at first—very few knew of my connection to April March. But once articles appeared in the papers, I became a bit of a local legend. I am eighty years old and sometimes it is hard to remember the sixteen-year-old starting out in burlesque. There is still more to April's story, but before we go any further, I want to talk about what happened to the important people in my life. Unfortunately, time passes—as do family and friends. There are so many who are no longer here. This is a tribute to them and what they meant to my life. I really loved them all.

My Grandparents

My grandparents raised me. I loved them and they loved me unconditionally. I feel badly that there isn't a lot more to say about them, other than that they were good people who worked hard to support themselves and me. They regularly had date night and would go out for drinks at a local tavern: my grandmother would have a beer and my grandfather would have two beers and a shot of whiskey. Then, they would come home. My grandmother said that they never had sex after my mother was born but I don't believe it. They fought frequently and hard, but were always tender with each other, especially in the later years when my grandmother fought cancer. My grandfather took such loving care of her that everyone who saw them was touched. My grandfather died at the age of eighty-two in 1968 in an Oklahoma City hospital. My grandmother died a few years later in 1971 at the age of eighty-five; she was in a home for the aged. In both cases, I was on the road and they died alone. I wasn't notified until sometime later.

My Parents

My parents' marriage didn't work, but they were still my parents. I loved them both, but was closer to my mother. She was a little more accepting of my career and we spoke frequently even when we didn't see each other. When I was dating Mel Torme, she put herself in the middle of the relationship. When I broke up with Mel, he went to see her in

California and asked her to help him get me back. She pleaded with me to go back to him, and I pointed out that she was my mother and ally—she should have been on my side. She wasn't, though, and thought I was nuts. I probably was.

My mother developed a drinking problem when she was in her late twenties. It would plague her for the rest of her life. She was the prettiest and most popular girl in town and everyone—including her—expected great things in her future. That didn't happen, though, and she was never happy or satisfied with her life. When she and Chuck Lillard settled in California, I began to realize that there were problems when I talked to her: her speech was slurred and she would repeat herself a lot, asking the same questions over and over. She showed symptoms of alcohol abuse that I usually ignored.

When I was young, she wasn't much of a drinker—so I just didn't hear what was right there in front of me. After a while, I said something about her drinking too much. Like other alcoholics, she became mad and insisted that she didn't have a problem. No matter how hard I tried, she wouldn't talk to me about why she drank or what was wrong. After admitting that she had a "little" problem, she stopped taking my calls. My grandparents told me that they were getting the same response, and we all were getting more and more worried.

Finally, one night I called and Chuck answered the phone. I bluntly asked him what was going on. After a long silence, he told me that my mother was ill. He said that she was very depressed and drank constantly. She was usually passed out on the sofa and wasn't functioning well, if at all. I asked to speak to her and he said that she wasn't there; he said he had no idea where she was. I felt so helpless: I had a young child and couldn't stop working to go to California. So, I called my father.

By this time, my dad had moved to Florida and had opened a service station. He had also remarried. That night, his wife answered and told me that my father had found out that I was in burlesque and was very upset with me and the situation. I asked why and she said that he was embarrassed about his daughter taking off her clothes in public. I told her that I didn't know how people would even know since I worked under a stage name, and that I was always disappointed with him for not being a real father to me. That was the end of that.

So, I had a mother drinking in California who refused to talk to me and a father in Florida who was angry at me because of my dancing. I also had two aging grandparents and a small child to care for and a career that was still developing. I had no one to rely on and help me decide what to do. Shortly after this, I married Charles Butler and he took charge. Thank God.

For a while, my mother seemed to be a little better and started going to AA. But one night, she called me, crying, and said that Chuck had left her and taken Patty Jo with him. Patty Jo wasn't his biological child but Chuck was the only father she had known so she willingly went with him. They were staying with Chuck's parents and, after hearing from my Mom several times, I called him. I knew that there had to be more going on than she was telling me. Well, there was. Chuck said that Mom was worse than ever and completely out of control. Her drinking and depression completely took over her life and he felt that he had done everything he could to help her. Finally, he said that he just had to get himself and Patty away from her. He told me he was filing for divorce and for the custody of Patty — he said that this time, he was really done. I told him that I understood, but I didn't know what to do. Charles and I talked about it for a long time and decided that we should have Mom come and stay with us in order to see if we could help her.

I was so excited about my mother coming to visit, and really thought that Charles and I could help. I also wanted her to see our home and to get to know Cyrese. I have to admit that I really wanted her to know that she was wrong about Mel, too, and to realize that I finally had a normal life. Charles and I cleaned the house of any temptation and locked all the alcohol in one out-of-the-way cabinet. We both met her at the train and quickly realized that she must have ridden in the club car from California. She was drunk, talking in slurred speech and could barely walk. Helping her was going to be difficult.

Once settled, my mother insisted that she had stopped drinking and was going to AA regularly. You could tell that this wasn't true just by looking at her. She also said that

Chuck was trying to get rid of her to marry someone else. After a few days, we settled into a routine and she seemed to be doing well. But then, Charles and I went to the Club for dinner one night and Mom wanted to stay home. When we got back, she had pried open the liquor cabinet and was out cold on the living room rug. In a few hours, she drank a quart of vodka and two quarts of bourbon. When I talked to her the next morning, she immediately attacked me. She told me that I was the last person that she would take advice from, and that I was a "former burlesque queen turned country club matron." She said that I wasn't very good at either.

So much pain from our tortured relationship came pouring out of us both. She told me that I didn't really know her and what she had gone through. She was right. We didn't know each other's pain and we had never really known each other. She always left me with my grandparents while she searched for her own dreams. I believe now that her carefree attitude and her continuous search for something else were covering up some deep pain. That day, I asked her—bluntly —to share it with me and she just turned away. Two days later, she went back to California, but Chuck and Patty Jo never came back to her. And her drinking continued.

After a few years, Mom and I started talking to each other again. I could tell that she was still drinking but I believed that I couldn't do anything about it. She was living with a retired gentleman and seemed to be doing okay. We didn't talk about anything real: we chatted like we were strangers.

I tried to help only once more: that time, I went to California. The man she was living with had told me how bad the drinking was and I came out again thinking that I could help. But I couldn't.

When I arrived, I found her sitting in the beautiful California sunshine, looking weak and frail. She was forty-three years old and there was no sign of the beauty she had once been. I told her that she looked well and she told me I was lying. We both laughed and sat and visited for a while. As soon as I saw her, I knew that she was dying and was determined to make the visit as pleasant as possible. I also hoped to get answers to some questions that I had about why she and my father divorced and about why she kept leaving me with my grandparents. Soon, though, I learned that she didn't have the mental clarity to answer these or any other questions.

My mom did tell me that she was proud of me and of how I "made it" in burlesque. She said that she never had the courage to follow her dreams, even though I never knew what those dreams were. While in California, I decided to take a few jobs to become known a little bit on the other coast. I made an appointment with Mr. Hal Morris at his Oakland office. It was intimidating just to sit there and wait: there were pictures of big stars like Tony Martin and Peggy Lee hanging on the wall. He represented them all, but I noticed that there were no dancers on the wall, and certainly no burlesque dancers. I was just about to leave when they called me in. I had dressed very conservatively in a business suit and blouse and low heels. Mr. Morris was very friendly and had a yellow parakeet on his shoulder. Yet, somehow, he didn't look strange. He asked if I was an actress, and when I said no. He almost immediately said that he could get me into a Contract School for ingénues at Columbia Studios. I told him that I was a burlesque dancer and that I wanted him to represent me for my bookings on the West Coast. He asked if I was sure about not going to Columbia and I responded that I was—I wanted to keep dancing. Anyway, the Morris Agency came to represent me and got me bookings at the Club Irisher in San Francisco and the Cliff House in Sausalito.

A few months after I returned East, I called to see how my mother was doing. Her roommate bluntly told me that she had died; he didn't bother to notify the family, and she was already cremated. She had died in April 1961 in California, at the age of forty-four. I was left with the job of telling my grandparents, Patty Jo, and Chuck, who still loved her. I adored my mother when she was young and so beautiful and exotic, and felt her pain as an adult as she disappeared into the abyss of alcoholism. This is why I seldom drink and still mourn this beautiful woman who never obtained her life's dreams and who I never really knew.

My father, Clarence (Buddy) Worden, was born on August 31, 1912 in Marion, West Virginia. He died in May 1974 in Miami, Florida. I didn't really ever know him either: I tried at times but we never connected. He hated that I was a burlesque dancer and never forgave me for it. Likewise, I never forgave him for leaving my mother and me, and for not telling me why. When I lived in Florida, he was really close by—but we only got together a few times and neither of us made any attempt to get together more often. Today, I say *what a shame*. Chuck Lillard never divorced my mother and was the real father to Patty Jo and me. He died of brain cancer in May 2009 in California. In his obituary, it stated that he was predeceased by his wife, Fern, and survived by his two daughters, Patty Jo and me. He loved my mother to the end. Bless him.

Jeffrey and Me

It is now 2016 and Jeffrey and I have been married for thirty-eight years. At first, we lived in my home in New Jersey. While in Jersey, we bought an RV and traveled to many different spots in the country. If we felt like going somewhere, we did. On our trips, we discovered that we loved the Adirondacks and the mountains of Upstate New York. So, we moved to Upstate New York. We bought property just a little north of Saratoga Springs and purchased our dream home, a log cabin in the woods. We have now been here for over twenty years and still love the area. Jeffrey has a private trucking business and still drives the east coast.

I had open heart surgery in 1997 in Albany, New York: I had the carotid operated on as well as two bypasses. Now, I have one Titanium Valve Replacement and must remain on

Coumadin for the rest of my life. I have back and leg issues that can't be addressed because of my other health issues. Considering all of this, I get along fairly well. I have a weight problem that I try to conquer religiously. We still have an RV and travel whenever we can; and, April March takes off every so often for some adventures.

Cyrese

Cyrese lives in Pennsylvania with her third husband. At various times, she has been a beautician, an acupuncturist, and an energy worker. She gave me the most precious gift of my life, my granddaughter Nicole. Nicole lives in Trenton, New Jersey with her husband, Matt, and is a makeup artist and hair stylist to many stars in New York City. We see each other often and talk all the time. She and her husband are so happy and I really enjoy spending time with them. I so hope that I am a better grandmother than I was a mother.

In 1965, I learned about what happened to Cyrese at the hands of Joe Marion. I was at home in Yardville, New Jersey when I received a call from Billy Ainsley. I had worked with Billy and his wife Levotus on the B&E Circuit and was very fond of them. Cyrese was friendly with their son and had told him the entire story about how Joe had raped her when I was on the Minsky Circuit. He told his parents, who then told me. Immediately, I confronted Cyrese about it and she lied and said that it wasn't true: she said that she had made the whole thing up. I was so angry that I slapped her, but much later I learned it was true. Cyrese had always insisted that it just wasn't so and I couldn't do anything about it. I found out about it well after I had divorced Joe, too. Much later, Cyrese would blame me for this and for being left alone so much. Our relationship really never recovered.

My Guys

I married a lot of men and was involved with a lot of others. I have no idea what happened to some of them, or even most of them. Even some of those whom I married, I have no idea where they are, here or there. This led to a funny story when I applied for Social Security: the man asked what my husband's name, social security, and birth date were. Of course, I gave him Jeffrey's information, but then he said that he needed the same data for anyone else I had been married to. I told him that I had no idea what the answers were to that question. He became very stern and asked me why not. Meekly, I told him that I had been married eight times. He just stared at me. Then, I asked how Social Security handled Elizabeth Taylor. He laughed, and I laughed, and together we figured out how to handle the problem at hand. A little humor usually goes a long way.

From what I know, Karl never retired from the Teamsters, staying with them at least on a part-time basis until he died. When I had my open heart surgery, Cyrese called him and told him that I was in the hospital. He called several times and we talked for hours. Finally, he told me that his wife was ill and that out of respect to her he wasn't going to call me anymore. We said our final, sad goodbyes. Karl was born in 1925 and died in California in August 2011. I will always see him in the stars and wish him love.

I think Manny is still alive and living in New Jersey. He never did divorce Helene and stayed with his family just as he should have. I loved him very much and still believe that I did the right thing. I would have been "the other woman" forever if I had stayed with him. We both would have lived in agony and unhappiness.

I don't know what happened to Charles. I did appear in Tulsa a few times after our divorce and always got publicity as a former golf champion. He never contacted me and I never called him. I still respect him and wish him well. If I could have been the normal wife that he had wanted, life would have been so different.

Benny remarried and had children with his second wife. I believe that they moved out of Oklahoma and that he died only recently. As for Mel Torme, he died in 1999 in California after a stroke. He had been married four times, once before we dated and three times after. He really was a brilliant songwriter and author. Also an author, he wrote a tell-all memoir of Judy Garland after working for her for a long time. When I hear the Christmas Song, I think of him: he wrote it sitting at his pool in the middle of summer. What a beautiful song it is. I also think of the words to his song, "Careless Hands." The first lines read, "I let my heart fall into careless hands." He did that with me. I was very young and he was ten years older. I didn't know what I wanted, but I am so sorry that I hurt him.

I have no idea what happened to the rest of them. It is a big country and they disappeared. Someone told me that Jack ended up in Florida, but I am not sure about that. The others still live on in my memory. May God bless and keep them all.

Jeff and me in New Jersey after I retired.

Jeff and me on our 25th Anniversary, March 2, 2003.

Jeff and our babies, Heidi and Tyler, in 2013. He was on Broadway in downtown Saratoga Springs; we love the location of our home.

Jeff and Heidi in York, Maine 2011. We still have an RV and enjoy road trips.

Here I am riding the Tram to the top of the Sandia Mountains in New Mexico, August 2013.

Nicole and her husband, Matt, at their wedding on the New Jersey Shore, September 2006. They are a wonderful couple.

Another picture of Nicole and Matt. I am so proud of them.

A picture taken in 1981 of one of the houses where my grandparents lived.

Another picture from 1981 of one of our stores.

A picture taken in 1981 of one of my grandparents' houses.

Here I am at my 70th birthday party on Saratoga Lake. It was June 2005.

My "Diva" golf cart. I loved the cart and playing golf.

BEND OF THE RIVER GOLF CLUB

Thursday Blind
Results, Aug. 14
First: Teresa Richard, Debbie Tobia.
Second: Kim Zilm, Ruth Lyons.
Tuesday Blind
Results, Aug. 19
First: (tie) Jim Hurley, Craig Brown (58); Bob Lyons, Bruce Stiles (58). **Second:** Mike Waterhouse, Kurt Long (60).
Ladies Club
Results, Aug. 20
Low net: April Edmiston (30). **Low gross:** Joan Draper (45). **High gross:** Mary Lou Baldwin (76). **Low putts:** Doreen Karcher (15). **High putts:** Norma Whitney (25).
Couples Club
Results, Aug. 22
First: Mona Wright, John Lyford (59 net). **Second:** Pat Welch, Shawn Darby (61 net).
Day/Night Tournament
Results, Aug. 23
First place, day pairs: Mike Waite, Diane Waite (45). **Second place, day pairs:** Tom Jordon, Scott Moore (49); Tink Wright, Mona Wright (49). **First place, night pairs:** Josh Gangaware, Marc Dewey (33). **Second place, night pairs:** Nate Cole, Marc Dewey (34). **Combination, day/night:** Josh Gangaware, Marc Dewey (83).

BROOKHAVEN GOLF CLUB

At the Red Hat meeting, where I had my coming out as a former burlesque star. The group made me so comfortable that I had gradually told them about my career.

Posing with my red gown. You can tell how scared I was by looking at my face.

With some of the ladies attending that lecture at the Wayside Inn in Greenfield Center, NY. This was the first time I had talked about burlesque in public.

My Name In Lights

During the early 1970s, I was known as "The First Lady of Burlesque" across the country. My name was on billboards and in newspapers across the land. Here I have included pictures of marquis and copies of some the articles and pictures that I saved from this period.

Publicity photos from
the early 1970s.

A picture of me at the Pilgrim Theatre in Boston, MA. This was just before the theatre closed.

The Town Hall Marquis in Toledo is shown on its last night of performances. Rose LaRose felt like I did about the changes in burlesque and closed her theatre.

Newspaper publicity for some of my
performances.

Exotic April March Stars
In Revue at Park Tonight

April March, a dark-haired beauty making her first appearance in Youngstown, heads the new revue opening at the Park Theater tonight.

Miss March is an established star on the East Coast, where she has appeared in the major burlesque houses. She was booked for the Midwest circuit of burlesque theaters following a tour of Europe, where she was a sensation in nightclubs from London and Paris to Berlin. She toured Europe for more than a year, one of the longest engagements for an exotic dancer on record.

Honey Darlin, billed as the "tall, torrid Texan," is co-featured in the revue. Patti Starr, remembered in Youngstown for her act with her famous sister, Blaze Starr, will make her first appearance at the Park in three years. Kippy DeVille, a favorite with Youngstown audiences, also appears in the show.

Comedians with the burlesque are Billy Foster and Phil McCabe, a straight man appearing at the Park for the first time. Foster and McCabe will introduce new material and specialty numbers in the show.

·April March

Youngstown Vindicator 25
Friday, November 1, 1963

PAGE 14   THE NATIONAL INSIDER

Strip Show Planned For TV

By SANDY RAINES

YOU MAY SEE APRIL MARCH on television in September of 1965. And the setting wil be in Florida, where it's warm, because April March is a stripper!

An independent company is reportedly being formed for the purpose of bringing out a series, probably the most daring ever produced for TV, titled "The Secrets of April March." Plans call for the show to be syndicated for late-night use, competing with Johnny Carson and Steve Allen, both of whom got the jump with belly dancers.

In an exclusive Insider interview, Miss March was reticent about disclosing what she knew of the deal — but did admit she had been approached.

"Actually, I'm not too anxious to do a television series," the voluptuous April said, "I'd rather go on Broadway as a dramatic actress, but I go where the money is."

We wondered out loud if she thought television was

ready for the proposed series, now that belly dancers were becoming commonplace.

"I really don't know, Sandy," she smiled, "but whatever they want I'm ready to do. In fact, I did belly dancing for a while. When Miami Beach declared strippers illegal, you know, I went to a choreographer and had some lessons.

"Then, after I had started doing the dance, the vice squad arrested me and hauled me into court on a charge of indecency. Can you imagine that?

"It sure made the vice squad look bad when the

Inside TV

judge released me," she mused.

"Things have been hectic lately, too. As you know, I was involved in a shooting at the Piggale in Miami Beach recently—that Korean.

"He confessed last week and they sentenced him to life. I'm relieved to know that I won't have to go to court or anything.

"I'm leaving for Europe in a few days," she went on. "I'm going to England, to

Manchester. For ten weeks, I'll be at Fox's Review Bar.

"It's a private club in Manchester, a sort of theatre-supper club thing. When I get back from there I'll know more about what I may do."

"Would you do your act on television, just as you do in burlesque, if say a Johnny Carson or a Steve Allen were to ask you?" I asked.

She smiled again, a most worthwhile effort. "Sure, if they'd want me to," she said brightly. "The exposure," she winked, "would be good for me."

"Do you really enjoy your work?"

"Sure, I do," the delectable one replied. "It's a good job, and I think every woman is more or less an exhibitionist. I know that people enjoy what I do, because I get real nice fan letters—and flowers, too. That makes a girl happy."

"How are you in the romance department?" That was a silly question, but she knew what I meant.

"I don't really have a boy friend. Oh, there is one fellow in New York—but it's nothing serious.

"It's not that I don't like men," she added hurriedly. "I like 'em very much, but I wouldn't want to be married

April March

again—at least not for a while."

"Are you ever bothered by sex crackpots, who might think you're a pushover for their advances?"

"No. None that I couldn't handle. Men are very nice to me, wherever I go."

"I suppose you like to be known as an exotic dancer?"

"I hate the word 'stripper.' It . . . it sounds so vulgar."

A copy of a scrapbook photo.

A copy of the article from
Sports Illustrated.

PEODL PEOPLE

"There is too much importance placed on winning," said sports-car enthusiast and hot pilot **Barry Goldwater.** But the front-running Republican candidate for nomination was not setting up an alibi for possible defeat at the convention in San Francisco; he was talking about participation in sports. "It's gotten," said Barry, "so you nearly have to be a professional to play anywhere."

Good old Silver has long since gone to that great pasture in the sky and Tonto is off somewhere clipping coupons, but even in retirement **Brace Beemer,** the last of the Lone Rangers (radio variety), can still cry "Hi Ho Silver!" and get an answer. In the corral of his 100-acre breeding ranch in Michigan, Silver's Pride, the 26-year-old scion of the equine star, happily munches hay and trots around regularly to be saddled by his master for a ride into the sunset.

Looking like a living odds-on bet, 5-foot-2-inch Harness Driver **George Sholty** and 7-foot-1-inch **Wilt Chamberlain** stood side by side and beamed at Wilt's 2-year-old pacer, Rivaltime, whom George had just driven to his fifth victory in five starts in Liberty Bell Park's Independence Pace. "I've been messing around with pacers for years," said happy Warrior Wilt, "but this is my first real good one."

It was a Texas-type story, even though it happened in Mississippi. Texas Football Coach **Darrell Royal** and Mississippi State University Athletic Director **Wade Walker** decided rather irritably to call off their golf match because of darkness after 14 hours of play and 60 holes. During the first three rounds, neither of the two old Oklahoma teammates had strayed out of the low 70s.

Ever since she picked up a set of men's clubs and learned the game, golf has done nothing but interfere with the true career of **April March** (née Velma Fern Butler), a 12-handicap attraction at New York's off-Broadway nostalgical *This Was Burlesque.* "Nowadays," complains April, "when I get written up, it is usually about my golf [*below left*] and hardly ever about my being a stripper [*below right*]."

The President of the U.S. feels secure enough to leave his hot

line behind in the White House when he plays golf. But when General **Thomas S. Power,** the Commander in Chief of SAC, goes onto the course he carries his phone with him, putting it down only to swing. Last week at the Offutt Air Force Base course in Omaha the 11-handicap golfer (who is also a black-belt *judoka*) received two calls. "That's nothing. We're usually interrupted more than that," said his playing partner, a three-star general who presumably has not seen *Dr. Strangelove.*

A confirmed water rat, Author **Richard Bissell** dragged his patient wife Marian off the comfortable quarterdeck of their houseboat *No Bottom* to board his tug, *Coal Queen,* for a three-craft Mississippi River race off Dubuque, Iowa. The eager *Queen* chugged into an early lead but, six miles and 35 minutes later, she crossed the line second by 10 lengths to *The Mary,* which, when not racing, pulls sand and gravel up the river. "We'll win next year," said Mrs. Bissell cheerfully. "This is gonna cost me a lot of money," groaned her crestfallen husband. "Now I'll have to buy new engines."

Onetime Welterweight Champion **Kid Gavilan** is reportedly serving a five-year term in Havana's La Cabaña Fortress for an unnamed political offense. What was he up to? Who knows? But soon after Gavilan left the ring he became a dedicated member of Jehovah's Witnesses and went back to Cuba to preach the Gospel. A sect that refuses even to salute the flag of a free republic is not likely to find much favor in Castro's Cuba.

Leaving the Philadelphia Orchestra to work out by itself for a moment, Concert Master **Anshel Brusilow** rushed over to supervise a practice session of his second concern—the first-place Cheltenham Township (Pa.) Little League baseball team. Unfortunately, the Pelicans' rehearsal was marred by

at least one sour note. "He fields well enough, but his batting is far from good," said Musician-Manager Brusilow, after watching his son David strike out for the second time. "I think he spends too much time at home practicing on his fiddle."

Palsy-walsy old **Nikita Khrushchev** likes to show that he's everybody's friend. And how better to do it than to join his buddies in their favorite sports? In Yugoslavia, for instance, he went shooting with President Tito. In Hungary he hiked with Premier **Kádár.** In Egypt he fished with President Nasser and last week in Sweden he was at it again. While Premier **Tage Erlander** made himself comfortable in the stern of a dinghy, the jolly Red crewman reached for the oars and rowed 300 yards across his host's private lake.

Sports-wise London newspapermen asked newly wed **Sir Frank Packer,** whose *Gretel* was the most recent unsuccessful challenger for the America's Cup, if his new bride shared his enthusiasm for boats. "She doesn't know the sharp end from the blunt end," responded the 57-year-old Aussie yachtsman. "She is strictly ornamental. And," he added thoughtfully, "a very good cook."

Pro golfers **Jay** and **Lionel Hebert** failed to make the cut at the U.S. Open, but they got a plateful of Congressional cold cuts in partial compensation when their namesake, Representative F. **Edward Hebert** of New Orleans, invited them for a lunch in a House dining room.

In Madison, N.J. **Mrs. Geraldine Rockefeller Dodge's** 49 dogs (mostly pedigreed) gobble up $50,000 worth of choice meats a year. Her court-appointed guardians tried to cut the bill to $14,000 a year, but Superior Court Judge Ward J. Herbert ruled that the 83-year-old heiress' pets should continue to live in the style to which she has allowed them to grow accustomed.

48

THE HOUSTON HALL BOARD

proudly presents

"GREAT EVENINGS IN THE THEATER"

Burlesque to Broadway

starring

MISS APRIL MARCH

and featuring

JADE GREEN   **PENNY CILLEN**

with

Johnny Crawford	Jerri Paris	Soo Ling
Maxie Furman	Ilene Hubert	Happy Bruno

Entire show produced by SAMUEL CAPPY and EDWARD A. RUDLEY

☆ Beautiful Girls

☆ Tassle Dancer

☆ Baggy-Pants Comedians

☆ Singer

IRVINE AUDITORIUM

※

Friday, February 10, 1967 — 8:30 p. m.

※

UNIVERSITY OF PENNSYLVANIA

WHO'S WHO IN THE CAST

APRIL MARCH began her career as a nightclub dancer eight years ago. Shortly thereafter, she was induced to try the art of striptease and became a star overnight after she was discovered by Harold Minsky who signed her at once for his "fabulous follies." Today Miss March is known throughout the world as the "first lady of burlesque."

MAXIE FURMAN'S life has ranged from his beginnings in Vaudeville dancing and comedy in 1928 to his present position as a burlesque comedy star. Mr. Furman starred in Mike Todd's production "Star and Garter Review" and later went on to play the lead in the USO production of "Mexican Hayride" during World War II. He has also appeared with the Minsky Follies in Las Vegas.

HAPPY BRUNO, this evening's Master of Ceremonies, was a motion picture actor at the early age of 14. He has appeared in Shaw and Lee's "Top Sergeant Mulligan" as well as several short subjects during the late 1930's. He was also in "Ken Murray's Scandals" (1941) before trading his tuxedo for khaki in World War II. During the War, he entertained our battle weary troops along with such stars as Bob Hope, Jack Benny and countless others.

ILENE HUBERT entered show business as part of one of the largest carnivals of the 1930's. She went on to become a top chorus girl and later, a highly regarded choreographer. Ilene, one of the best straight women in burlesque today, has also toured the country with her late husband, George Murray.

PENNY CILLEN is a statuesque young lady who started out to be a physical education major at the University of Arkansas but found a better use for her talents in the field of burlesque. She is reputed to be one of the best tassel twirling dancers in the business today.

JADE GREEN, a resident of the Philadelphia area, began as an exotic dancer in the night clubs of New York City. Three years ago she changed her style from the exotic dancing required at the clubs to that type of striptease that is known to please a theater audience and entered the world of burlesque. She is beautiful, intelligent and considered to be a fine straight woman.

JOHNNY CRAWFORD is one of the top young singers in the business today. He has several records to his credit and has appeared in some of the finest nightclubs in the United States. He is the author of the show's theme song, "Wonderful World of Burlesque."

JERRI PARIS first began a career of show business at the Palace Theatre in San Francisco which was followed by several movie parts and night club engagements. Jerri is a Philadelphia native and maintains a large following in this area.

SOO LING is a master in the arts of magic. She uses the audience as part of her show and involves them whenever possible in her act. She gives away canaries, removes garments from people in the audience and has men tearing up money. She has entertained thousands and continues to be a popular performer.

SAMUEL CAPPY and **EDWARD A. RUDLEY** (Producers) are well-known throughout the burlesque world. Mr. Cappy has worked as a singer and straight man as well as a producer. Mr. Rudley, a Philadelphia attorney and alumnus of Temple University, is legal representative of theaters extending over half the United States.

Chapter Nine

The Rest Of The Story

I really thought that I had retired from burlesque for good. Burlesque was an art of intrigue: but when I retired in 1978, there was little intrigue left in the shows. Burlesque had become stripping: you went down to your birthday suit. That wasn't me. And honestly, I was just past forty and getting too old for stripping. Did I miss it? Yes, I did, very much. But did I want to strip? NO! I never considered myself a stripper. So, retired I stayed.

Jeffrey and I moved north from New Jersey, first to Corinth, New York, and then to Wilton, just north of Saratoga Springs. It was the mid-1990s, and we slowly settled into our new lives. I had sold most of my burlesque costumes and had thrown out all of my contracts. Still, it was hard to move forward when I so missed the past. Then, all of a sudden, there was a renewed interest in burlesque and its role in our country's entertainment history. I was on the fringes of this and didn't expect to be part of the "New" Burlesque movement.

Two years after my open heart surgery, I was thankful that I was alive and could play golf again. I belonged to the Bend of the River Golf Club and was in Ladies' Leagues and doing well. I had my own golf cart—black with purple stripes. I also had purple clubs and a purple bag and a license plate on the cart that read "April." My touch for the theatrical carried over into golf. I joined a Red Hat group (popular in the 1990s) and played weekly in a Mah Jong Group. I still missed burlesque, but had built a nice life for myself. I even lectured at some local groups, telling them about my life in burlesque. I showed my scrapbooks, pictures, and the few costumes that I still owned and talked about my experiences.

In 1999, I received a call from Jane Briggeman in Las Vegas. She had located me through an old friend from burlesque, Carmella Rickman. Carmella and I had maintained sporadic contact over the years and she knew where I was and how to reach me. Jane was planning a burlesque reunion in Las Vegas and wanted as many of the old stars as possible to come. It was scheduled for the Gold Coast Hotel in June. I immediately accepted the invitation and was so excited. I couldn't wait to get together with all of my old friends. Once there, I reconnected with a comic named Jimmy Matthews. It was so wonderful to see him. From that time until he died, we kept in close contact through telephone calls, letters, and visits when I was in Vegas. Jane started hosting reunions regularly and I went to each one. I also started teaching a class for the younger Vegas dancers called "The Elegant Strip Tease." It was and is quite popular.

I have had so many amazing things happen since then and I am so thankful for these experiences. At the age of seventy-six, I had my picture in Penthouse magazine in an article about burlesque, as well as my story and picture in a recent article in British Airways magazine. I have also done interviews on BBC radio and television channels. I met a woman named Leslie Zemeckis in the early 2000s — and life took off from there. I met Leslie through Barry Sigfried and Dorothy Coleman. Dorothy and Barry went to the same camp in the Poconos as Cyrese and her husband, and when Cyrese mentioned that her mother was April March, she learned that Barry's mother had been in burlesque, too. Dorothy had been handling the press issues for Leslie on a documentary that she was doing on burlesque and Leslie called me soon after and introduced herself. She asked me to come to New York City to participate in the filming of *Behind the Burly Q.*

I took the train to New York City and was so nervous. Cyrese met me when I reached the city and together we went to the Four Seasons Hotel to meet Leslie. That day, I spent over five hours filming for Leslie and we soon became friends. For the movie, Leslie was gathering information from former burlesque stars and doing extended interviews with each one that she found. She was excited about the project and her enthusiasm was contagious.

After the New York taping, Leslie asked me to come to Las Vegas to participate in a program that was taking place at the Stardust Hotel. Leslie had asked Jane Briggeman to host another burlesque reunion to film for part of her documentary. Many of the old timers came; Alexandra the Great 48 and Val Valentine were there. It was so, so good to be with them again. My first meeting with Alexandra the Great 48 was almost fifty years before. I was performing at one of my favorite theatres, The Town Hall in Toledo, Ohio. Rose LaRose, one of the most famous burlesque stars of all time, owned the theatre. Rose and I were friends and she made a flapper for me to wear only in Toledo. There was a piece of material in the front that swayed when you bumped, revealing almost everything. Underneath, there was an expanded g-string contraption with jewels on it that bounced when you moved. It was quite daring and such fun.

One night, Rose invited some of us to go with her to see a show in another club. She was interested in signing one of their performers and wanted to see what we thought. Well, this absolutely beautiful woman came on stage: she looked like a young Sophia Loren. Her act, too, was amazing. We all agreed that Rose should hire her and she did. Rose named her "Alexandra the Great 48" (because of her bra size) and she went on to star in the best clubs all over the world. We all stayed friends and kept in touch throughout the years. We loved these reunion shows, as they allowed us to spend some time together on a regular basis. Alexandra now lives in Texas and runs a very successful beauty care line. Her products are all that I use.

The first reunion took place in 2007 and after that they were held on a regular basis. I went to *Behind the Burly Q*'s 2010 premier in New York City and appeared in a similar documentary titled *Burlesque Uncovered* shortly after. It took Leslie four years to complete her film. When it debuted, it was immediately critically acclaimed and was eventually picked up by Showtime. It still airs frequently and is the best background piece on burlesque. In addition to former dancers, many of the comics appear in the movie. For instance, Alan Alda talks about his experience in burlesque theatres when he was a boy. His dad, Robert Alda, was a successful straight man in the shows and he had wonderful memories of living with the performers while growing up.

After the documentaries, even more people started asking me to come to their groups and talk about burlesque. I did radio shows with Leslie to promote her movie and the book that followed. Some even asked me to teach dancing and to show audiences how to "shimmy like their sister Kate." All this interest made people start to think about reunion tours and—lo and behold—they came to be. So, there I was at the Miss Exotic World Pageant in 2009, onstage and doing a burlesque routine. I got a standing ovation, and I loved it again. So many emotions came over me on that stage. The adrenaline was pumping and I felt so much younger. I wanted to be part of the burlesque revival and explain the profession to others. I felt that because of the stripping it had earned a bad name; burlesque was so much more than stripping. No matter how badly I felt, all my worries would disappear when I would go onstage: I'd get into character and I'd feel so much better.

Soon after, that pageant was renamed the "Burlesque Hall of Fame" and became a yearly event. A wonderful lady, Laura Herbert, had taken it over and moved it from the desert into town. She introduced me to Grant Philipo, who had started a Las Vegas Showgirl Museum with memorabilia from the past and present. The weekend is now held in June at the Orleans Hotel. All of us who can attend go every year and it is wonderful. Later in 2009, I also performed in the Boston Burlesque Exposition and was inducted into the Canadian Burlesque Hall of Fame. I am the only American that has received this award.

During this time, I met two wonderful men who became very important to me. And no: I didn't marry either one of them. The first is Grant Philipo, the Las Vegas producer who owns the Las Vegas Showgirl Museum. He has choreographed all of my routines and designed my costumes over the last several years. He also had the song "Roxy" from the Broadway show *Chicago* rewritten for me. It is called "April," of course. When I go to Vegas, I always stay a few extra days with Grant and his partner, Mary Dee Mantle, and we have so much fun. One of my favorite parts of our visits is when we stay up talking all night and then drive downtown in our pajamas for donuts and coffee. His museum is amazing: if you ever have a chance you should go. You will have a wonderful time.

The second is a film producer, Craig Jackson, who is making a documentary about my life in burlesque. The film is called *Becoming April March* and it is almost completed. Craig has been filming me since 2012 and has filmed my act in Las Vegas twice. He has visited my home and filmed our daily life. One time, he even taped me getting a cast removed from my ankle after a serious bone break and then followed me as I went to physical therapy to rebuild my strength. He has film of me at the New York City Festival in 2014, too.

In June 2015, I was named "Legend of the Year" by the Burlesque Hall of Fame. It was the highlight of my career and such a special night. Craig filmed the entire show and Grant designed my costume and routine. He also had six young, scantily-clad men from the show at Bally's perform with me and assist me with the striptease. This was the first time that I performed to the song "April" and it was a success. It was a surprise that Alexandra the Great 48 came to Vegas to present the award. Laura Herbert, the woman that brought me to the Exotic World of Burlesque and introduced me to Grant years ago, gave me the trophy and my wonderful granddaughter was there to share the evening with me.

So here it is February 2016. It is freezing in northern New York and I am sitting in front of my fireplace thinking of these last sixteen years that have meant so much to me. I have upcoming events scheduled in Vancouver, Oklahoma, and, of course, Las Vegas. This book should come out at the end of the summer of 2016 and the film released in 2017. It is so nice to know that people recognize my contributions to burlesque. I have reconnected with many and made so many new friends. It would be impossible to mention all of them here. But I do need to send special thanks to Leslie, Grant, and Craig, who have helped bring burlesque to the attention of a new generation and have explained it so eloquently. I am so blessed to have you all in my life. To the fans that come to my shows, I adore you all. Some walk through life knowing only a few, but I have danced through life knowing many. Hopefully, this dance will go on forever.

With Nicole just before my first burlesque appearance in thirty-one years.
We were at the Plaza Hotel in Las Vegas.

This is from my first meeting with Leslie Zemeckis in New York City. Her camera
person, Sherry, is with us; we were filming for Behind the Burly Q. This interview
and my friendship with Leslie would change my life.

Cyrese came with me to meet Leslie. I was so nervous. I hadn't talked a lot about my years in burlesque and this interview was to be included in the major documentary, Behind the Burly Q. I even brought one of my few remaining costumes with me.

Leslie and me getting ready for the premier of the movie by doing a radio interview on April 23, 2010 in New York City.

At the premier of the movie, with Leslie and her husband, Robert Zemeckis, a well-known movie producer, and my granddaughter Nicole. The premier was at the Quad Theatre in NYC and we all felt like movie stars.

This is from a group reunion at the ribbon cutting for the new Burlesque Hall of Fame Museum in Las Vegas (2013). Tempest Storm is next to me on the left.

With a few of my burlesque friends in Las Vegas.

This is at the Boston Expo in April 2012. I had a table set up to sell
my photos and t-shirts. What a great time!

At Grant's home in Las Vegas with a group attending one of the reunions in 2013.
I love our times together.

At the Boston Expo in 2011 with a group of friends and former dance students.
Montel Williams' ex-wife, Grace is on the right next to me.

Craig Jackson, filming *Becoming April March*. I hope the movie will be released soon.

Two of my dear friends from Montreal, Canada,
Bert and Nathalie. This was taken in 2012.

At home in 2014 rehearsing my number for Las Vegas and doing
a last minute costume check.

The Burlesque Revival

Over the last several years, I have participated in a revival of burlesque. I have again performed, taught classes about the dance and its techniques, and lectured to classes of adults and students about burlesque. This chapter includes pictures of some of these performances and my new publicity shots. I have loved each and every moment of this movement and thank God for the opportunity to be a part of it.

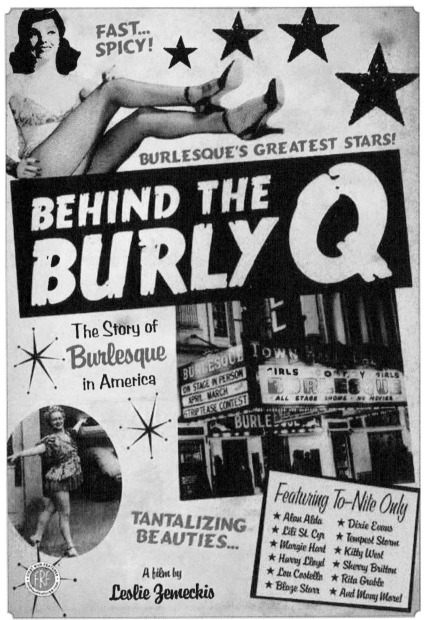

A copy of the book jacket and DVD cover of Behind the Burly Q, a film and book that brought new attention to the art of burlesque.

BEHIND THE BURLY Q

The Story of Burlesque in America

"Leslie Zemeckis has preserved for us a lively, lovely corner of American life." -Richard Schickel, Film Critic & Historian

Burlesque was one of America's most popular forms of live entertainment in the first half of the 20th century. Gaudy, bawdy and spectacular, the shows entertained thousands of paying customers every night of the week. And yet the legacy of burlesque is often vilified and misunderstood, and left out of the history books. By telling the intimate and surprising stories from its golden age through the women (and men!) who lived it, *Behind the Burly Q* reveals the true story of burlesque, even as it experiences a new renaissance.

"Absorbing, moving...the stories are rollercoaster rides!"
-Emily Hourican, Irish Independent

OPENS APRIL 23 IN NEW YORK CITY
QUAD CINEMAS
On 13th Street Bet. 5th & 6th Aves • 212-255-8800 • www.quadcinema.com
1:00; 3:00; 5:05; 7:05*; 9:45 *Filmmaker Q&A after Fri & Sat 7:05 Shows

OPENS MAY 7 IN LOS ANGELES
LAEMMLE'S SUNSET
8000 Sunset Blvd • West Hollywood • 310-478-3836 • www.laemmle.com
Filmmaker Q&A Opening Weekend! Visit laemmle.com for details.

A MISTRESS, INC PRODUCTION PRESENTS A LESLIE ZEMECKIS FILM
ORIGINAL MUSIC BY PHIL MARSHALL EXECUTIVE MUSIC PRODUCER JOEL SILL
ASSOCIATE PRODUCER DONNALEE AUSTEN EDITED BY EVAN FINN
DIRECTOR OF PHOTOGRAPHY SHERI HELLARD EXECUTIVE PRODUCER ROBERT ZEMECKIS
PRODUCED BY SHERI HELLARD AND JACKIE LEVINE
WRITTEN, PRODUCED AND DIRECTED BY LESLIE ZEMECKIS

For filmmaker appearances, trailer, and more info visit
www.firstrunfeatures.com • www.behindtheburlyq.com

New headshots of a former burlesque star.

Here I am posing with Leslie and Robert Zemeckis at the New York City Premier of *Behind the Burly Q.* What a wonderful night.

Nicole and me at the rehearsal of
my first show in 31 years.
This was in 2009 at the
Orleans Hotel in Las Vegas.

This picture was taken in 2009 in
Las Vegas before my performance.

A photo taken during a performance in 2014 at the Albuquerque Burlesque Festival.

Here I am performing with Jett Adore at the Burlesque Hall of Fame at the Orleans Hotel in June 2014.

Few know just how elegant the costumes we wore were.
Various conferences have displayed these gowns.

This was taken in 2008 at the Boston Burlesque Expo at the Cambridge Hotel.
My red costume is in the Burlesque Museum.

This picture shows my white gown and undergarments. This was one of my
favorites. It showed off my dark hair and olive skin perfectly.

This photo is from the Boston Expo in April 2009.
The gown in the middle was one of mine.

This is Alston Stephanus. I met him at the VIP Party for the
Burlesque Hall of Fame Meeting in 2013. It was at the Orleans Hotel in Las Vegas.

Here I am with Mysterion and Wolfman at the Toronto Burlesque Festival in 2014.

With Nicole and Grant at the Las Vegas Showgirl Museum.

Dressed and ready to perform in Las Vegas.

Me posing with my costume at the Festival in Toronto Canada in January 2011.

Being escorted onstage by Grant in June 2015. I was named Legend of the Year.

Here I am with Julie Mist and Alexandra the Great 48 in Las Vegas in 2015. Alexandra is my best friend; I love her like a sister.

Alexandra and me on the same night.

From my number at the BHOF in June 2015. Grant arranged for the dancers.
The young men were very talented. Really.

Receiving my award from Alexandra the Great. What a night that was!!

The "Legend Walk" at the Orleans Hotel in Las Vegas.

Conclusion

Like many, I have found myself in my later years. I am at peace with Velma and April. I realize that there are two sides of me and I respect them both. Life has been good to me. I loved all the men that I was involved with — at the time at least. I know some are still alive and some have passed on. I want them to know that I loved each and every one of you at some point in my life. I hear Karl's and my song "I Wish You Love" when I think of each of them. I hope they know that they are always in my prayers and thoughts.

To all of my friends and family, I appreciate your support and love throughout this incredible journey. I have shared my life with you. It has been one hell of a ride all these years. And to you, my readers, I say, "Regrets, I had a few, but then again too few to mention. But, through it all I've done it my way."

And, the beat still goes on. Thank you all.

Love,

Appendix

My Husbands

First Loves	*Marriage Dates*
1. Benny Mitson	1950-1951
2. Jack Johnson	1952-1954

Short-lived	
3. Glenn Quick	1954
4. Fred Jhan	1955

And Four More	
5. Charles Butler	1956-1963
6. Joe Marion	1964-1974
7. Joey Ross Jr.	1975-1976
8. Jeff Edmiston	1978 to Present

I really loved my first two husbands and when I married I thought it was for life. When I quit burlesque to have Cyrese, I believed that Jack and I would be married for ever more, and that Cyrese would have the life I didn't have with two loving parents.

The next two marriages were really rebound relationships. I never expected either to last and still hoped to reconcile with Jack, at least for Cyrese's sake.

The next two were attempts to find a normal life, although I didn't really know what that meant. My marriage to Joey was more of a business arrangement, and a good arrangement it was. My marriage to Jeff has lasted and no one is more surprised than Jeff and I.

I have been married to Jeff for 38 years.

Burlesque Clubs I Worked

Alabama
Port Said, Birmingham, AL

Arkansas
The Old Dutch Inn, Little Rock, AR

California
New Follies Theatre, Los Angeles, CA
Rio Follies Theatre, Sacramento, CA
President Theatre, San Francisco, CA
Follies Theatre, San Francisco, CA

District of Columbia
Celebrity Room, Washington, D.C.
Frederick's, Washington, D.C.
Gayety Theatre, Washington, D.C.
Paper Doll Club, Washington, D.C.
The Plaza Theatre, Washington, D.C.
Silver Slipper, Washington, D.C.

Florida
Club Copa, Cape Carnival, FL
Torch Club, Fort Lauderdale, FL
The Clover Club, Miami, FL

Florida (continued)
Picadilly Club, Miami Beach, FL
Place Pigalle, Miami Beach, FL

Georgia
Peachtree Club, Atlanta, GA

Kansas
T Bone Supper Club, Wichita, KS

Kentucky
Savoy Theatre, Louisville, KY

Maryland
Gayety Theatre, Baltimore, MD

Michigan
Empress Theatre, Detroit, MI
National Theatre, Detroit, MI
Wood Six Theatre, Detroit, MI

Missouri
Grand Theatre, St. Louis, MO

New Jersey
500 Club, Atlantic City, NJ
Capital Theatre, Atlantic City, NJ
Globe Theatre, Atlantic City, NJ
Jockey Club, Atlantic City, NJ
Hi-Lite Club, Kingston, NJ
Pier One Supper Club, Toms River, NJ

New Mexico
Hymie's Club, Albuquerque, NM
Pop Bar Inn, Raton, NM

New Mexico (continued)
Raton Club, Raton, NM

New York
42nd Street Theatre, New York City, NY
Broadway Burlesque, New York City, NY
Mayfair Theatre, New York City, NY
Hillside Theatre, Queens, NY
Civic Follies Theatre, Syracuse, NY

Ohio
State Theatre, Canton, OH
Gayety Theatre, Cincinnati, OH
Roxy Theatre, Cleveland, OH
Mayfair Theatre, Dayton, OH
Geneva Theatre, Geneva on the Lake, OH
Town Hall Theatre, Toledo, OH
Park Theatre, Youngstown, OH

Oklahoma
Gaiety Theatre, Oklahoma City, OK
Louie's 29 Supper Club, Oklahoma City, OK
Jake Samara's Derby Club, Oklahoma City, OK
Rio Theatre, Oklahoma City, OK
Stage Door, Oklahoma City, OK
The Stardust, Tulsa, OK

Pennsylvania
Lyric Theatre, Allentown, PA
Troc Theatre, Philadelphia, PA
Casino Theatre, Pittsburgh, PA

South Carolina
Gayety Theatre, Myrtle Beach, SC

Virginia
Lee Theatre, Richmond, VA
Texas
Theatre Lounge, Dallas, TX
Matin's Melody Lounge, Houston, TX

Out of Country Engagements
Casino Theatre, Toronto, Canada
Lux Theatre, Toronto, Canada
Victory Theatre, Toronto, Canada
Arthur Fox Review, England
Tivoli Club, Juarez, Mexico
The Follies, Juarez, Mexico
Lobster Trap, Halifax, Nova Scotia

Theatre Ensembles:
Ann Corio
B&E Circuit
Minsky Shows
Quaker City Follies

The Official

April March Cocktail

2 ounces Aged Rum
1.5 ounces Framboise or Raspberry Liqueur
The juice of 1/2 lime

Pour the ingredients into a cocktail shaker filled with ice. Shake. Do a little dance in honor of the First Lady of Burlesque. Shake some more, then strain into a chilled martini glass. Garnish with a single raspberry slit with a pairing knife so it fits easily on the rim.

Historical Notes

The following provides additional information about some of the important characters in my story. They all played an important role in my life. In addition, they made their own important contributions to history.

Saud of Saudi Arabia

Saud was the King of Saudi Arabia from November 1953 until November 1964. At a very young age, he was named the successor to his father, King Abdul Aziz. He died in exile in 1969. He was known for bringing some order to the government and developed numerous plans for improving the country's infrastructure. He reigned during a very political and tumultuous period, yet he established numerous ministries and a university in Riyadh. He was determined to leave his power to his sons. In 1957, the United States caused the fall of oil prices in the region and the relations between our two countries became very strained. This may have been the reason for the secretive letter that I gave him. I will never know. He had 115 children and numerous wives. He believed in the education of women: one of his daughters became the first female president of a Saudi School. https:// en.wikipedia.org/wiki/Saud_of_Saudi_Arabia

Minsky Revue

Minsky's Burlesque Revue was created by four brothers in 1912. The early shows ended in 1937 in New York City. The shows were considered obscene and lewd in their time. Now, they wouldn't even raise an eyebrow. At first, Minsky's primary audience was poor immigrants and many believed that it made them forget their plight for a little while. For a small admittance fee, you had a few hours of escape and entertainment. The brothers also offered many comics a gateway into show business. These included Phil Silvers, Zero Mostel, Morey Amsterdam, Red Buttons, Robert Alda (Alan's father) and Red Skelton. They also premiered many Burlesque Stars, such as Lili St. Cyr, Gypsy Rose Lee, and Ann Corio. The brothers believed that a good striptease dancer had to know the exact moment to remove each garment. They treated it as an art, not just going on stage and taking off your clothes. Most of their stars started stripping in their teens and earned between $700 and $2,000 a week. One of the brother's adopted son, Harold, kept the shows active through the 1960s and brought many first-rate comics and burlesque stars to their stage. He is responsible for bringing their stage to Las Vegas and reaching the upper-middle class crowd. The revue ran for many years to large crowds. Harold lived in Las Vegas until his death in 1977. It was Harold that I worked for many times. He was a true gentleman. http://www.burlexe.com/burlesque/burlesque-history/ burlesque-theatre-minskys-burlesque

Arthur Fox Revue, Manchester England

Arthur Fox was known as Manchester's King of Glamour. As early as 1947, he was touring striptease shows all over England. His show was England's Minsky Revue. The club in Manchester was opened in 1959 and was known as the most glamorous nightclub in England. He was determined that only burlesque "stars" would appear at the Club. After I performed there, he always listed my name first as one of his international headliners. He wrote his autobiography and self-published it under two different titles, "Striptease with the Lid Off," and "Striptease Business." His story was that of burlesque in England. http://pamela-green.com/arthur-fox-manchesters-king-of-glamour/

Ann Corio

Ann Corio was born in 1909. While still a teenager, her looks and body shape landed her showgirl roles. Rather than becoming a movie star, she became a top striptease artist. Her rise to star-status started in 1925 and she was soon on the stage in Minsky's Burlesque. She was also well known for performing at the Old Howard Theatre in Boston, Massachusetts. It was said that every male college student in that lovely city was in love with her. She had a long successful career on burlesque stages across the country. In 1962, she put together the off-Broadway show called *This Was Burlesque*. She later wrote a book of the same name. I was proud to have been in her show. The show also went on the road for several seasons and did not close for good until 1985. Its last stage was a dinner theatre in Florida. Of the many stars and comics that appeared on her stage, Ann took special credit for grooming Lou Costello into a star. She was proud of her career and of burlesque until the end. She died in 1999. http://www.imdb.com/name/nm0179875/

Lili St. Cyr

Reporter Mike Wallace called Lili St. Cyr "the highest paid striptease artist in America." Of all the important people he interviewed, he admitted that he was most fascinated with her. He felt that her beauty and poise were magnets that just drew you in. She had an incredible life and career and was married six times (two fewer than me.) She also had romances with stars such as Vic Damone and Yul Brenner and was named one of the ten most beautiful women in the world, along with Ava Gardner and Brigitte Bardott. In the 1950s, she was the most famous woman and the face of burlesque after Gypsy Rose Lee and Ann Corio retired. Props were an integral part of her act. In addition to the bathtub, she had wedding, Cinderella, and virgin skits. But there were also dark spots in her life: she was arrested numerous times for indecency charges and made a number of suicide attempts. She was incredibly shy and, at times, looked very frail. With her husbands, she spent her savings quickly and she was poor and reclusive in her older years. She died in 1999 in Los Angeles under her birth name, Willis Marie Van Schaack. She is the subject of a new biography, *Goddess of Love Incarnate*, written by my friend Leslie Zemeckis. Lili herself was also my friend and I treasure our shared memories. http://www.imdb.com/name/nm0820506/bio

Leslie Zemeckis

Leslie Zemeckis is an actress, writer, and award-winning documentarian. She is also the guardian angel of the Burlesque Revival and my friend. Leslie co-wrote a one-woman show entitled "Staar" and is the author of the book and producer of the film, *Behind the Burly Q*. The film still airs on Showtime. The film reveals the never-told stories of the men and women who worked in burlesque during its Golden Age and is the definitive history of burlesque and its stars. As a writer, she has published articles in many magazines. She has also produced a documentary called *Bound by Flesh*, the story of Siamese twin superstars Daisy and Violet Hilton. This film played to sold-out audiences at numerous film festivals across the country. Her most recent book, *Goddess of Love Incarnate*, is the story of legendary burlesque star Lili St. Cyr. http://lesliezemeckis.com/biography

Author's Note

I met April a few years ago at a beauty salon. Isn't that where ladies are supposed to meet? I had run in to drop something off at my cousin's shop and April was sitting there having her hair done. I sat down and started talking to this beautiful woman and we hit it off right away. We were joking and laughing with each other in a matter of minutes. Like many casual contacts, we said we hoped we would see each again and went our separate ways.

About a week later, I received a call from my cousin's husband who said that April really wanted to talk to me. He asked me to call her as soon as I could. It seemed that April had been trying to find someone to write her story for a number of years and had run into one obstacle after another. I had told her when we met at the shop that I had written our family's history and had written a lot of materials for the government program where I worked. I was cautious about this new project, but her enthusiasm won me over. After a bit, I said that I would do it.

This is the simple story of how a really strange partnership was born. April's story is one of strength, determination, and endurance. She kept going no matter what. She was a burlesque star, married eight times, traveled all over, and was known internationally as the First Lady of Burlesque. I went to small Catholic schools, never married, and developed programs for seniors in New York State. We were and are two opposites. But, we were two kindred spirits that were meant to meet and were drawn together by a project that we both believed in. Like April, however, if someone offered me $10,000 to give me a bath, I would say yes: so we may not be that different after all.

This book is based on hundreds of hours of conversations that took place while sitting around April's kitchen table and a wealth of background materials and photographs that she kept from her career. It was and is a privilege to know her and to have worked with her on this book. I hope you enjoy her story.

April March

Acknowledgments

There are so many people that I need to thank for making this book possible. First, there are my family and friends who have supported me through this process. I want to send special thanks to my husband, Jeff, and my granddaughter and her husband, Nicole and Matt Eventoff. They keep me going when I want to stop and stop me from going too far when I stray. Also, Gerri Weise (Alexandra the Great 48) has stayed by my side for over fifty years. We talk weekly and see each other whenever we can. My life is so much richer with her in it.

Secondly, this book would not have come to life without the work of Susan Baird. She is smart and hard working, and makes any situation happier and easier to get through. There were several false stops to this effort that delayed the project for over five years. Susan stepped in and kept it going until it was finished. She stayed focused and gave the book form and life. During this time, we became close friends. I treasure her support, guidance and ability to get things done. I am sure she will remain a very important part of my life.

Then, there are Craig Jackson and Grant Philipo. They came into my life when I most needed them and took me on a journey that was hard to imagine. Today, they both are family to me, family that I love very much. Craig is like Peter Pan. He sprinkled fairy dust on me and made me fly again. His movie, *Becoming April March*, will soon be finished and released. It is a wonderful tribute to me and to burlesque. I encourage you to see it when you can. Grant has developed new routines and costumes for me. He supports me in all of my performances. He is always there and has my back as the kids say.

I want to thank ShiresPress, in particular Debbi Wraga and Aubrey Restifo, for their help in publishing the book. And, special thanks to all of my fans who have waited so patiently for this book. I especially hope that you enjoy it.

Finally, I send thanks and prayers to Karl, my lost love. Many, many years ago he told me, "Sweetheart, you should write a book about your life. It has been really something." Well, my dearest, I finally did and I did it my way.

CPSIA information can be obtained
at www.ICGtesting.com
Printed in the USA
BVOW07*0048080916

461190BV00003B/2/P

9 781605 713274